GOD
OF OUR MOTHERS

GOD
OF OUR MOTHERS

Face to Face with Powerful Women of the Old Testament

M. R. RITLEY

MOREHOUSE PUBLISHING
Harrisburg, Pennsylvania

Unless otherwise noted, the Scripture quotations contained herein are from the New Revised Standard Version Bible, copyright © 1989 by the Division of Christian Education of the National Council of Churches of Christ in the U.S.A. Used by permission. All rights reserved.

"The Parable of the Old Man and the Young" by Wilfred Owen, in *The Collected Poems of Wilfred Owen*, edited by C. Day Lewis, New Directions Publishing Corp. Copyright © 1965 by Wilfred Owen. Permission sought.

"Sisters, Sisters," from *White Christmas* (Paramount, 1954). Words and music by Irving Berlin. Copyright © Irving Berlin Music Company. Permission sought.

"Kingsfold" by Ralph Vaughan Williams, from *The Hymnal 1982*. Copyright © 1985, Church Publishing Incorporated. Permission sought.

"She Comes with Mother's Kindnesses," words by Kathryn Galloway, in *Music for Liturgy, 2nd Edition* published by St. Gregory of Nyssa Episcopal Church, San Francisco, CA. Used by permission.

Morehouse Publishing, P.O. Box 1321, Harrisburg, PA 17105

Morehouse Publishing, 445 Fifth Avenue, New York, NY 10016

Morehouse Publishing is an imprint of Church Publishing Incorporated.

Cover art: *Eve* by Lucien Levy-Dhurmer. Courtesy of Giraudon/Art Resource, NY

Cover design: Laurie Klein Westhafer

Library of Congress Cataloging-in-Publication Data

A catalog record of this title is available from the Library of Congress.

Printed in the United States of America

06 07 08 09 10 9 8 7 6 5 4 3 2 1

To the woman whose courage gave me life,

whose genius for friendship taught me how to live,

and whose humor has echoed in the laughter of all my days,

MY MOTHER
Ella Nogrady Ritley
(1913–1989)

CONTENTS

Acknowledgments ix

Introduction
Goodbye to "Father Knows Best" 1

Chapter 1
Still Friends with God: The Eve No One Remembers. 11

Chapter 2
Family Values in Abraham, or
". . . and Baby Makes Four" 27

Chapter 3
"The Mother of All Believers": Hagar's Journey to Freedom 47

Chapter 4
The Invisible Man and the Managing Woman, or
"Mother Knows Best" 61

Chapter 5
"Sisters, Sisters . . .": Sibling Rivalry to the Max 81

Chapter 6
Ruth and Naomi: "Getting by with
a Little Help from Our Friends" 97

Chapter 7
Judith: The Woman and the Warrior 115

Chapter 8
Esther: Genocide, Faith, and the Whole Megillah 133

Chapter 9

Our Lives, Our Stories: Being God's Women Today................147

Appendix 1

Some Tips for Study Group Leaders................................151

Appendix 2

Study Guide Materials..153

Notes...163

ACKNOWLEDGMENTS

This book has been so long in the thinking, the teaching, and the slow coming-together that I hardly know where to start in my acknowledgments.

At the outset, there were the women at St. Augustine-by-the-Sea, Santa Monica, who helped me struggle my way to a new spiritual identity: Barbara Harrison, Shirley Webb, and the Revs. Marni Schneider and Carlyle Gill. As they would say: "The nerve of those women!" When I moved on to Holy Nativity Parish, Westchester, the Rev. Martha Siegel helped me rediscover my gifts as a teacher, and above all has never ceased encouraging me to return to my writing. I thought of all these women more often than I can say during the writing of this book.

The actual start of these portraits of God's women—and men—begins with Lisa Neufeld, whose friendship now reaches through over thirty years of my life, who invited me to teach at the Family Weekend for Temple Akiba, Culver City, in 1990. Rabbi Allen Maller and the congregation proved how special they are by inviting an Episcopal seminarian to teach a class on biblical men and women for a synagogue gathering!

In 2000 and 2001, I presented the first versions of the class, "God of Our Mothers," at St. Gregory of Nyssa, San Francisco, and St. Paul's, Oakland, as part of a joint education venture planned for both parishes by the Revs. Rick Fabian, Donald Schell, and Jack Eastwood. All the students in these classes (both men and women, by the way) helped shape this book with their questions and comments, but the one whose forthright humor was most notable—and even the memory of whom kept me going during this book's writing—was, of course, Norma Harrington. I miss her more than I can say.

Through Sharon Seliga, another one of my St. Gregory's students, in September of 2002 I had the privilege and delight of sharing these stories with a group of spirited Lutheran women from St. Paulus's and St. Mark's churches, San Francisco, at a weekend retreat in San Anselmo, California. Their lively responses to these stories gave several of them new dimensions for me.

Finally, in the fall of 2004, the Rev. Kathleen Van Sickle encouraged me to start teaching again after a two-year hiatus, this time at Good Shepherd Episcopal Church, Berkeley. The group that gathered in our "Tent of Teaching" in the parish hall added more to the class than they can know. They ranged from teenagers to women in their eighties, clergy and lay women, lifelong Bible readers and brand-new churchgoers, and their insights into the stories were unbelievably diverse.

It was during the presentation of this class that Debra Farrington of Morehouse Publishing saw the ads for it in our parish e-mail newsletter and asked if I thought there was a book in here. Thanks to her and to Nancy Fitzgerald, senior editor at Morehouse, *God of Our Mothers* finally began to come together at last.

A special thank you should go to Kathy Galloway, Leader of the Iona Community in Scotland. I first became acquainted with her wonderful hymn, "She Comes with Mother's Kindnesses," at St. Gregory of Nyssa, San Francisco, where it was sung (as she intended) to the tune *Martyrs*. At one point I wanted to use it for a service, sung to the tune *Kingsfold*, but it didn't fit the tune, so I shamelessly (and without permission) tucked another half-verse in to make it fit. She has graciously given me permission to print her verses, along with my step-verse, to the tune of *Kingsfold*, for which I am grateful!

As a last note, I have to thank the women whose modern-day stories form the ending of each chapter. Some of these were gathered from classes and workshops, others from interviews and e-mail. They were taped, told aloud, or written down, and I use them with the kind permission of the women who gave them to me. The names and some details have been changed, but the stories are alive with the very individual voices of some of God's most memorable women.

INTRODUCTION

Goodbye to "Father Knows Best"

THE OLD TESTAMENT ACCORDING TO NORMAN ROCKWELL

I'll admit it up front: the most vivid pictures I have of the Old Testament women don't come from the Bible at all, much less that well-laundered version of the Bible dished up to small children in Sunday School in the '40s and '50s. The pictures I remember are Hollywood at its best—or worst. Hedy Lamarr as Delilah, for instance, showing a great deal more skin than any respectable religious woman in my neighborhood even admitted to having; or Anne Baxter with her bosom heaving mightily over Moses before he got to talking to burning bushes.

Yes, well, they were Hollywood, and we more or less understood that they weren't *really* real, anyway. But at least they were more interesting than the Sunday School versions of the same women, who certainly weren't depicted as having bosoms, heaving or otherwise. They were depicted as— well, let's face it, dull.

I remember one Sunday School book I had when I was about eight or so, in which little Jacob and his sister Miriam helped their family settle the Promised Land. Little Jacob, I recall, got to do interesting things like watch his father repel the Canaanites from a well; little Miriam helped her mother grind barley. And smiled about it. Jericho fell—"Hurrah!" went little Jacob, seeing it from afar. Little Miriam, busy grinding her barley that day, missed out on that one, but she just kept smiling. And so it went. Little Jacob got to hear Joshua exhorting the Israelites. Little Miriam got to help Mom grind the barley.

I was pretty sure little Miriam was getting the fuzzy end of the lollipop in all this, but then again, I figured with a mother that agreeable, she didn't have much choice. Biblical Mom was unfailingly sweet, supportive, and cozy.

1

I wasn't sure what the women in my family would have made of the invasion of the Promised Land, but I found it hard to picture them being quite that placid and opinionless.

> *You want to build a boat in our back yard and expect me to go along and clean up after four decks of livestock? Sure, honey, no problem.*

> *God wants you to take this son of mine that I waited ninety years for and go offer him up on a mountain? Sure, honey, and what would you like me to have ready for supper when you get back?*

Maybe it was like that in other people's neighborhoods, but I somehow couldn't picture the women in my family being quite that agreeable. Obviously, Sarah, Rachel, and Rebekah never lost their tempers with their husbands or yelled at their kids, but I figured, with God looking over their shoulders, their style was somewhat cramped. And obviously they never sweated, swore, or looked as if they'd spent the day wrestling a bunch of kids in and out of their baths.

It doesn't take any stretch of the imagination to see why a fair number of women went looking for another religion as soon as they were old enough to. One where, hopefully, they wouldn't end up grinding the barley while the guys got to do all the interesting things.

Without being too facetious, I think it's safe to say that a great many of us were handed pictures that were remote or difficult to identify with: the perfect and glamorous Hollywood women, or the perfectly ladylike Sunday School ones. Many of us, of course, were afraid to admit that we couldn't identify with these paragons, or the God who seemed to think they were the greatest things since kielbasa and sauerkraut. But we knew something was out of sync with the real-life women we knew.

And there you have it: the women of the Hollywood and Sunday School versions bore little or no resemblance to the real women most of us knew. The women in my family and my neighborhood, for instance, were Eastern European immigrant women who knew what life was like at its toughest. They were good people, but they were flawed and real, peasant women with earthy senses of humor and a direct, forceful way of expressing themselves. They talked back: to their husbands, to the pastor, to the saints, even to God on occasion. I remember one of my father's aunts, a devout Orthodox woman, scolding St. George in no uncertain terms for falling down on the job after she'd spent days praying. "And you! Aren't you ashamed of yourself? If *your* mother was asking this, you'd see to it!" (I suspected she was privately planning to have a word with St. George's mother, and St. George probably knew it, too.)

Even if the women in our families were more polite in style, they were also women who were *real* and found ways of making their feelings and their opinions known, whether the subject was the invasion of the Holy Land or the conduct of the local pastor.

Sadly, we were left with the impression that there was something wrong with the real women we knew or grew up to be, not that there was something wrong with the pictures of women we were shown in the first place.

Even worse, neither Sunday School nor Hollywood ever told us there was such a thing as a dysfunctional family, or that several of them played prominent roles in the Old Testament (which we'll see when we look at Abraham's family, or Rebekah's). Nobody ever hinted that the godly people in the Old Testament could be dishonest, manipulative, and conniving—and still be chosen and acceptable to God. You might have found yourself thinking—with some justification, too—"God, I wouldn't buy a used car from Jacob or Laban," or "Why is Sarah treating that poor Egyptian girl that way?" But we wouldn't have voiced the thoughts back then.

The High Price of Reality

Once Sunday School days were past, and I got out of the church setting, I began to discover that my suspicions were not only true, but quite perceptive: biblical women really weren't like that. Many of the scriptural versions I'd been shown were distorted and unreal, and sometimes downright sinister. I began to understand that the social and gender decks were decidedly stacked, and that much of real life simply got trimmed out of the Scriptures. Like many of us, as I became acquainted with the insightful and challenging feminist studies of Scripture, it became fairly obvious that these were patriarchal documents that were stacked in favor of men, documents that over the centuries had been used as a major instrument of the oppression of women, as well as other minorities.

Many women find a great and heady sense of freedom in that recognition, an acknowledgment that their own perceptions had been more accurate than anyone had been willing to admit, and that there was nothing wrong with them or the women they grew up with. The wrongness lay instead in a distorted—and often demonized—view of women, handed down generation after generation, until the reality of women's lives became invisible, *even in full view*. The freedom of reclaiming our own reality and history is, however, a mixed blessing for many of us. The cost of reality is staggeringly high at times. One of the costs is that we can no longer turn to this document for the strength and assurance we may have found in it earlier in life. The passion of the Psalms and the prophets is forever after tainted with the suspicion of their patriarchal origins and message.

As I, for one, became more schooled in post-modernist thinking, and the process of deconstructing texts, the problem presented by the biblical text grew both clearer and more opaque. Trained to read with a certain amount of suspicion, I couldn't read the Scriptures without asking, "Who wrote this and why did they tell the story this way? Why did they include this? Why did they leave that out? What was their agenda? Who benefited from this way of telling the story? And who was left out, who was disenfranchised and stripped of humanity and power?"

Unsurprisingly, I often found myself thinking back to little Miriam in my Sunday School book, relegated to grinding the barley while the menfolk shaped history to suit themselves. Or thinking, "Poor Sarah! She thinks she's nobody unless she produces a male child!" and "Look at what they've done to Hagar, who has no choice as to whether or not she'll bear a child for another woman, and then gets thrown out into the wilderness so her son won't inherit along with the ruling class!"

It all made sense. It all needed saying. But underneath all of that, part of me grieved at losing any possibility of finding the faith and love I had earlier found in the Scriptures. In moments of great grief and crisis—and there have been many over the years—I envied the passionate certainty that the women of my childhood seemed to have in reciting the Scriptures. But I also knew I couldn't go back to that passionate naïveté again. I knew too much.

So here I was, marooned in a kind of no-woman's-land, unable to find a bridge between the Scripture that had been a life-giving text for millions of people (including women) for centuries, and the modern and post-modern readings that opened my eyes and freed my mind but often left my heart and spirit curiously empty. (All right, I'll admit it. As a gay woman, I find that deconstruction comes easily to me, but it doesn't do anything spiritually *creative* for me, either.)

Deconstruction nurtures my mind, not my heart. I'm a creative person who needs a certain strength to create, and I must find what gives me that strength. Deconstruction doesn't provide it for me. This isn't evidence of my flawed nature. It wouldn't have done much for my Aunt Magda, either. We're basically peasant women: our needs grow out of the earth. So, at the risk of sounding deplorably incorrect (and I've been that most of my life anyway) I have come to admit that I can't deconstruct my way into a life of living faith, a spirituality that gives *me* life. And I don't think I'm unique in that.

What I'm saying is that *by itself* literary deconstruction isn't enough. Yes, it's important that we deal with it, and it's opened important insights up for me and for millions of other people, both men and women. But as much as we've gained, we've also lost something vital in that process, and we must somehow reclaim it.

RECLAIMING THE DEEP ROOTS

I come from a working-class immigrant family in which Scripture was undeniably a major source of strength in a very tough life, something you turned to for the hope and tenacity to go on. Patriarchal or no, the Psalms, the prophets, and the stories themselves were springs of life in barren ground for the people of the inner-city neighborhood I grew up in. Non-English-speaking, unskilled immigrant men didn't rule the world, either: they could also be its victims. The women in the family and neighborhood around me were not the weaker helpmeets of all-wise and all-powerful men, but the towers of strength who kept their families together when the factories were closed or the foundry shut down or the men were out of work and out of heart.

They had the strength to talk back—even shake their fists and scream back—at life's unfairness, and the courage to persist in that until they were able to find their feet again. I needed to find my feet again, my roots in that world, too. I was beginning to ask myself, "How can I go back and reclaim the strength of those stories in a way that makes sense to me, without going back to the Little Bo Peep version of the women in Scripture I heard in Sunday School, or the uncritical acceptance of patriarchal attitudes?"

Something interesting happened along the way that became a kind of talisman for me. I was a seminarian, doing my obligatory stint of Clinical Pastoral Education at a Veteran's Administration hospital in Palo Alto, California, and struggling with multiple issues of how to find a place for myself—my *real* self—in the church. I couldn't picture myself as a chaplain in a military setting, given my history of protesting the war in Vietnam. I didn't see any role models who looked or felt like me.

Then one afternoon, I was called to anoint an elderly veteran who was semi-comatose and clearly dying. Armed with The Book of Common Prayer and a vial of holy oil, I found myself in a hospital room, looking down at a stranger who was hovering on the very cusp of death. What on earth would a real chaplain feel, or do? I wondered.

Unexpectedly, I suddenly felt myself surrounded by the women I knew from my childhood, when people still died at home and had their eyes closed and their hands folded by the women of the family. They were suddenly with me, my mother, my aunt, my mother's godmother, the woman from across the street, and I knew instantly who I was and what I was there to do. I held an old man's hand and recited the twenty-third Psalm, laid my hand on his forehead to comfort and reassure him as he balanced in that lonely place. I felt his life slip away, and I felt the deep peace of knowing we were both surrounded by a great cloud of witnesses.

In the end, the presence and reality of the women I grew up among outweighed any speculations, any theories, any doubts. It took me through the rest of that summer and the rest of seminary. It took me back to the Scriptures, in the company of women who talked back, asked questions, and weren't afraid either to laugh or to cry at what they saw, heard, and knew.

A New Way of Traveling

Here, then, was my own personal journey, set out in front of me, a way of traveling back through the layers of knowledge and naïveté. I could go back to the Scriptures themselves and re-read them in the company of those real women I had known. And suddenly, I began noticing things I hadn't seen before, and I thought, "Wait a minute! I don't remember this! Why didn't I notice this before?" For instance, every time Sarah opens her mouth and tells Abraham to do something, Abraham's response is, in effect, "Sure, honey. Anything you say, honey. What do you want me to do, honey?" Why did I never notice this before? It's there, and as I began to re-read it, I saw it: she opens her mouth, and Abraham jumps to do it. He never challenges her. What patriarch left *that* in? Is it possible that some of the patriarchal editors weren't really any sharper than my Uncle Zóli, who always let Aunt Szófi have the final word? (I noticed it because my Aunt Szófi would certainly have noticed it.)

Or take another example. Abraham sends his servant to bring a wife home for his son Isaac. But who is actually in charge of making that match? Well, everybody in Rebekah's family speaks up *except Dad*. The only thing he says in this whole account is, "Take her and go." *What?* This is the patriarch of the household? It sounds like he's just sitting in the corner while the rest of the family does all the talking. Was he hung over that day? Or was he just used to the fact that nobody paid much attention to him? Was Rebekah such a pain he just wanted to get rid of her? What's going on here? Even without specialized knowledge, it's easy to see there's something odd here, and that this isn't the ideal biblical family we were taught to think was there.

Now, I'd been raised on these stories. I thought I knew them! Sharp little Jacob hoodwinks his father and has to run away from his brother. Except that, in re-reading it, I realized that Jacob wasn't sharp enough to dream that one up. Rebekah was pulling all the strings. "You go here, you do that, you just leave this to me." And Jacob does exactly as she says. She knew perfectly well Esau wasn't going to kill Jacob: she clearly had another agenda, and she was very clever at bringing it to pass. This woman was definitely in charge of her menfolk, and when she wasn't, she set things in motion to make sure that she was. Yes, I could see the real women I knew in that story, and they weren't behaving as the patriarchal agenda said they should!

When Patriarchal Slips Are Showing

So I had to start asking myself, "Wait a minute! If this is a patriarchal document, how did these little tidbits get in here in the first place, and how did they get *left* in here? Who slipped up? Where did they come from?" They're clearly authentic, because they're often the most lively and real things in these stories. You walk into the house of Rebekah, look at the characters, and can't help but think of dysfunctional families you've known and loved—

and maybe lived in. If this were a twenty-first-century home, Rebekah would be hanging out at the mall to see what interesting things are going on, and Laban would be the wheeler-dealer who has a closetful of car stereos that fell off the back of the camel. Dad's given up trying to cope with the family, and even Mom has taken a backseat to her kids.

Clearly, family values in Abraham aren't what the religious right thinks they are.

I strongly suspect that some of the answers to these puzzles are simple and direct. When we look at Scripture, we're looking at a document whose composition starts at about 2000 B.C.E.—about four thousand years ago. It started as an oral tradition, and it was actually centuries before any of these stories were written down. True, when the time came to write them down, the writers were probably all men. *But the stories had been told for centuries before that, and where did the men get these stories in the first place?*

Who told the stories? Who spent most of their time with the children to begin with? In this culture, even male children spent the first seven to eight years of their lives exclusively with the women. So who told them the stories? Of course, it was Mom and Grandma, and their aunts and great-aunts, and Mom's best friends, the women they grew up calling "Auntie." Isn't that how most of us learned our family stories? No matter who wrote the stories down, you can still detect the voice of somebody's aunt talking about their grandmother.

> *"When your great-grandmother was thirteen the Russians burned down most of their village, and she and her little sister Rivki only escaped because they'd been out in the thicket gathering wood for kindling. They hid under a pile of brush at the edge of the field all that night,"*

or

> *"This was a really small town, and we were the first Chinese family who ever lived there. The first day that Auntie Fan went to school, even the adults from the store came over and stared in the windows at her because they'd never seen a Chinese girl before except in the movies,"*

or

> *"Did you know your Dad's grandmother was only nine when she came here all alone on the boat from England? Her relatives had pinned a tag to her coat that said, 'Please see this girl gets to her father, Mr. Jim Parrish, Locust Street, Johnstown, Pennsylvania. He'll pay you.'"*

This is what *God of Our Mothers* is about. It's about recapturing the stories of real, live women with real lives, not the too-good-to-be-true women of the Sunday School books or the every-hair-in-place women from TV and Hollywood, but women who fled from the Dust Bowl to the migrant work camps, or welded Liberty Ships together in the Richmond shipyards, or raised their children in half-burned homes along the path of Sherman's March, or arrived at Ellis Island with everything they owned in bundles. How many of us have stories like these in our families—not necessarily dramatic, or heroic, but real? Stories that someone told us when we were little?

> *"Grandpa was already in this country, working in a coal mine in West Virginia, when the house where Grandma was living burned down. So she took the two kids, tucked them in a pushcart with an old down comforter, and started walking till she got to Budapest, where she had relatives. They lent her the fare to get here. She couldn't speak English, and she couldn't read or write. All she had was the envelope of the last letter Grandpa had written to her, and she just kept pointing to his return address, trusting that people would get her onto the right train and get her off at the right stop. And sure enough, he came up from his shift in the mines one afternoon, and there's his wife and two kids waiting for him."*

What was the message most of us got from these women? *"Survive. You do what you have to, you raise the kids, you see to the meals, you close the old folks' eyes when they die. You pray a lot, and in the meantime, you work."* In my family most of the women worked in factories or in hotels or as waitresses; in families that lived on farms the women certainly spent as many hours a day milking cows and hoeing beans as the men did, plus having to cook meals and nurse sick kids, doing whatever they had to do. Even in families whose economic lives were far better, they were the steady strength at the heart of things, who dealt with family crises and unexpected sorrows, day in, year out.

Those are the women whose stories we will actually find in the Old Testament. These aren't women in Norman Rockwell families, but women left in awful situations, like Ruth and Naomi, who have to use all their ingenuity to work things out. Some of them—like Hagar—aren't what your grandmother would've called ladies, but their stories are the stories of real women, and they shine through even the patriarchal overlay.

Moreover, their stories are universal. The first time I taught some of this, I actually taught it at a family weekend for Temple Akiba in Culver City, California. I think it was the only synagogue who had an Episcopal seminarian leading a class. I heard stories from women whose grandmothers and great-grandmothers came to this country as picture brides, to build lives, to build families, and did it with strength and humor—and sometimes with a lot of pain, too. That's what these stories are about.

Granted, this won't necessarily read like the usual adult religious study text, but then, I've always had a suspicion that if God had wanted me to be as polite as little Miriam, grinding her barley with a winsome smile, I wouldn't have been born Hungarian, in Cleveland. It was, perhaps, as close as she could get me to the kind of women whose stories are found in the Old Testament, and I honestly believe the women of the Old Testament would recognize my voice as theirs, and claim me as one of their own.

So here, then, are God's extraordinary women, and what I hope will be both a surprising and spiritually nurturing look at the real God of Our Mothers.

CHAPTER ONE

Still Friends with God:
The Eve No One Remembers

THE PATCHWORK BIBLE

There was a time when this part of the chapter probably wouldn't have been necessary—or maybe even possible. If you were raised the way most of us were, the Bible was simply the Bible, that book that sat on the shelf in the parlor, or on the lectern at the parish church. Your granddad (like mine) may have read a chapter of it aloud every morning, and the expert, whether priest or minister, preached about it on Sunday, but either way, it was simply the Bible, and that was that. Mostly, you were simply expected to listen up.

I do recall having to memorize large chunks of it in Sunday School, and earning a colorful little sticker for every verse I managed to recite back. Since this was in the days before most folks knew what the word "relevance" meant, and I had a pretty good memory, I can't recall being too upset at not understanding a great deal of what I memorized. After all, kids are constantly up against things they don't understand. In a bilingual family like mine, it's hard enough sorting out which words belong in what language, much less worrying about words nobody ever said in real life anyway. Like most of my classmates, I quickly tumbled to the fact that John 11:35 was the shortest verse that would get you a sticker ("Jesus wept."), and that you wanted to stay away from books like Nehemiah, which were just jammed full of unpronounceable names. Beyond memorizing, or hearing it preached about, most of us weren't encouraged to ask too many questions about the Bible. It was there. It was itself. It was IT. And that was that.

For some of us, it came as a great shock to discover that the Bible isn't simply IT—a single book—but a whole collection of them, many decidedly user-unfriendly, and a number of them an editor's nightmare (or at least the work of some of the sloppiest editors in history). The fact is, the original writers had no idea they were creating *Scripture*, particularly since the idea of Scripture didn't yet exist. They wrote things down from a sincere and genuine belief that it was important to preserve these stories, rules, and insights for others, but they didn't figure what they were writing would become untouchable. Their heirs didn't have that idea, either, and set about merrily improving the text (is there a writer or editor alive who doesn't believe they can make it better?), or rewriting it to fit their own ideas of what was important to preserve. It didn't become untouchable—unrevisable—until it had been centuries in the revision, and there was no possible way on earth of reconstructing the original.

The literary smorgasbord we call the Old Testament, which contains a little something for everyone, ranges in age from oral traditions dating back at least to 2000 B.C.E.[1] to tightly crafted literary works written just a few hundred years before Christ. It spans social, religious, and political developments from the traditions of families or clans of wandering herders and traders, to the royal archives of typical late Iron Age kingdoms in the Middle East, to the cosmopolitan world of Hellenistic Alexandria. It's the work of family storytellers, royal archivists, pious lawgivers, and rebellious visionaries. For every Isaiah, capable of poetry that lifts us to the breathtaking vision of God's awesome mercy, there's at least one earnest bureaucrat dithering over language that's specific enough to hold up in court. How all of these writings manage to coexist in a single volume is possibly the greatest miracle since the parting of the Red Sea. But it's a very human miracle, the work of countless scribes, retellers, editors, and preservers.

Eve: Shuffling—and Unshuffling—the Deck

You could say the Bible is sort of like a deck of cards, made up of different suits. The folks who put it together shuffled the cards up and called it a book. It's hard to tell what suit any Bible story comes from until you turn the cards face up and unshuffle them. Let's begin with the story of the first of our mothers, Eve. It isn't the work of a single storyteller, but at least two of them, and they tell two very different stories—neither of which is actually the one most of us expect to find when we turn to Eve's story.

Most of us think we know the story, whether we heard it in Sunday School, from Sister Mary Stanislaus, or from popular wisdom: God made Adam, and then took one of Adam's ribs and made Eve. And everything was fine in Eden, until the Devil came along, disguised as a snake, and talked Eve into sinning, which screwed up the rest of the world for all time. That's the story most of us have heard. Sound familiar?

The interesting thing is, it's not the story we can actually find in Genesis. Or perhaps I should say, there's a story in black and white in your Bible that will probably challenge what you think you know about Adam and Eve. Let me also say in advance that, even when you discover that you can't find the story you thought was there, it's remarkably hard to shake its influence. I've had students who have kept obstinately searching for the pieces they *know* must be there, long after it becomes apparent that they simply aren't.

So. Let me begin by pointing out that in the other two religions that share this story—Judaism and Islam—*neither sees Eve as the source of evil in the world.* Only in Christianity do you get that. In Islam, there's no idea of original sin. We're all born innocent, the thinking goes, and we sin only when we're old enough to understand and choose to disobey God. We can't hang it on Eve, Adam, or anyone else. In some Islamic traditions, in fact, the faithful believe that when a child is born, God and all the angels hold their breath in delight and awe: perhaps this will be the child who will never turn away from God and will never sin. I love that picture of God and the angels all agog, hoping this will be the one. It sure beats the notion of being conceived in sin and born in iniquity.

In Judaism it's the same: babies are born innocent, and children are just children. They have to learn what's good and bad, what's right and wrong, and they're not morally responsible until they're old enough to understand. Only then can they be considered to break God's laws or be capable of doing evil.

So in Judaism and Islam, Eve doesn't carry the burden of introducing sin into the world. Each person is responsible for doing good or evil.

But in Christianity, something very different—and very unfortunate—happened. When the Roman Empire in the West collapsed economically and politically, most of what we call civilization went with it. That included literacy, the making and reading of books, and the functions of law and education. What remained of those things was mainly preserved and carried on in monasteries—a mixed blessing at best. It was decidedly a good thing that the literature and learning of the ancient world were preserved in some fashion. It was unfortunate that it happened to be in monasteries, because monasteries, after all, are all-male communities, and that had some peculiar effects on the way Scripture was read and interpreted.

Up till the time of the Reformation, it was common for families to dedicate young boys to the religious life at ages as young as three and four. These child oblates, as they were called, were turned over to monasteries to be raised by the monks. For the rest of their lives, they had little or no contact with women, or even ordinary family life. They may have glimpsed the village women who came to the parish mass, but these would have been mainly peasant women—illiterate, certainly not educated or refined. Or else they saw pristine images of the Virgin Mary in church, a woman who was *always* a virgin—as they were supposed to be, too.

In other words, real women were as unknown to them as the inhabitants of Tibet. Moreover, women represented something dangerous to the chaste monastic ideal. They were, after all, sexual (*gasp!*), a real threat to men who were trying to maintain an ideal of chastity. No wonder they saw women as sinister sources of temptation and evil! This is not only the idea that permeates most of later Western religious culture, but it forms the original lens through which the Church tended to read the story of Adam and Eve thereafter. Needless to say, in this crowd, Eve was operating under a distinct handicap.

Christianity had another problem with defining where sin started, and how contagious it is. If people aren't born in sin, early Christians wondered, what are the Incarnation and Crucifixion about? In other words, why was Jesus born as a human being in the first place, and why did he die on the cross? Most Christian theology starts with the assumption that Jesus was born into this world only because fallen humanity needed a savior.[2] Suffice it to say, this didn't do Eve much good, either.

As we begin to read the text of Genesis carefully, we may notice that this theological and monastic veil is still clouding our vision, making us think we see things in the story that really aren't there. So pay attention, because much of what you learned in Sunday School about Eve simply isn't in the Bible.

Let's begin by looking at the outline of how the story is put together from at least two different sources.

GOD CREATES THE WORLD—TWICE

We begin with Genesis 1:1, where most of us are on familiar ground. "In the beginning, God created the heavens and the earth," and so on. Whether we're Bible readers or not, it's a line most everybody knows.

This first version of the creation we encounter in Genesis is probably quite late—it was written around the time of the Babylonian exile, only six centuries or so before the birth of Christ. During their long years of exile—from about 597 till about 539 B.C.E., several generations of Hebrews were exposed to a powerful civilization and a sophisticated public religion with large temples and impressive ceremonies.

One of the things we may notice about the first creation story in Genesis is that it almost seems written to be read in a ceremonious manner. It is not only poetic, but almost musical, like a hymn or anthem with a repeated refrain. It repeats and repeats and repeats. "God said, 'Let there be . . . . and there was. . . .' God said, 'Let there be light'; and there was light. And God saw that the light was good, and God separated the light from the darkness. . . . And there was evening and there was morning, the first day" (Genesis 1:3–5).

Now comes the next repetition: "And God said, 'Let there be a dome in the midst of the waters, and let it separate the waters from the waters. . . . God called the dome Sky. And there was evening, and there was morning, the second day" (Genesis 1:6–8).

This is pretty sophisticated imagery, not the work of a primitive storyteller. This is a poet at work. "Then God said, "Let the earth put forth vegetation: plants. . . . And there was evening and there was morning, the third day." (Genesis 1:11, 13)

By this time, even if we've never heard this before, we know what to expect—just like little kids listening to a bedtime story. By the second repetition of ". . . then I'll huff and I'll puff . . . " the kids can already shout, ". . . *and I'll blow your house down!*" And how they love doing it, too! Because, in the simplest way, it means they *own* the story now.

In this creation story, something similar happens, and it's masterful storytelling. Most Hebrew people didn't have the written text in front of them, but after a few repetitions, they had a familiarity that assented to a line like ". . . and there was evening and there was morning, the fourth day." It's how we come to *own* texts.

This isn't a primitive story. It's a theologically sophisticated literary work; God is bringing things into being by simply speaking, by the power of the word alone: "Let there be!" "And there was!"

> And God said, "Let there be lights in the dome of the sky to separate
> the day from the night." . . . God made the two great lights—the
> greater light to rule the day and the lesser light to rule the
> night—and the stars. . . . And there was evening and there was
> morning, the fourth day. (Genesis 1:14–19)

Keep in mind that the sun and the moon are the primary deities in Babylon, above all the others gods and goddesses. With a mere flick of the wrist, the writer of Genesis has just made all those other gods subordinate to the God of Israel. It's remarkable to see a conquered culture asserting itself and saying, "But our God created the Babylonians' gods. Our God is above them."

So creation continues along in this way, all the plants and animals are brought forth, until we get to Genesis 1:26:

> Then God said, "Let us make humankind in our image, according to
> our likeness; and let them have dominion over the fish of the sea, and
> over the birds of the air, and over the cattle, and over all the wild
> animals of the earth, and over every creeping thing that creeps upon
> the earth."
> So God created humankind in his image,
> in the image of God he created them;
> male and female he created them. (Genesis 1:26–27)

Notice that there is no gap between the creation of male and female. The first time humankind is spoken of, it's as "them," not "him"—a simultaneous creation of male and female, *both* in the image and likeness of God. No mention of ribs at all.

So all is created, and on the seventh day, God rests, and there's a nice little coda. Look at Genesis 2:4: "These are the generations of the heavens and the earth when they were created."

It's right there, at the end of that phrase, "when they were created," that the editor of Genesis changes from one version of the creation to another version. The editor doesn't pick up this first strand again until Genesis 5:1. If you skip ahead to it, you'll see that it's simply a continuation:

> *This is the list of the descendants of Adam. When God created*
> *humankind, he made them in the likeness of God. Male and female*
> *he created them, and he blessed them and named them*
> *"humankind" when they were created. (Genesis 5:1–2)*

What intervenes between Genesis 2:4 and Genesis 5:1 is the second version of creation. You can see at once how much more primitive it is.

THE MUD-PIE VERSION OF CREATION

Creation: The Sequel begins at the second part of verse 4, "in the day that the LORD God made the earth and the heavens, when no plant of the field was yet in the earth and no herb of the field had yet sprung up" (Genesis 2:4–5). We've already skipped over some of the days of creation, where God made the plants and fields, and gone back to a more primitive version.

> . . . *[F]or the LORD God had not caused it to rain upon the earth, and*
> *there was no one to till the ground; but a stream would rise from the*
> *earth, and water the whole face of the ground—then the LORD God*
> *formed Man from the dust of the ground, and breathed into his*
> *nostrils the breath of life; and the man became a living being.*
> *(Genesis 2:5–7)*

It's not only much more primitive than the earlier part of Genesis, it's much more typically Middle Eastern. Humanity is created as a kind of little mud pie. That's where the name Adam comes from—the root word *adamah*, means earth, making the first man the "Earthly One"—Dirt-Man, if you like. He doesn't really have a name yet when God creates a garden and puts the Earthly One in it.

Now at last all the plants spring up, and the river comes out of Eden. "The LORD God took the man and put him in the garden of Eden to till it and keep it," as if God has just created the first maintenance staff (Genesis 2:15).

Nothing here about the image and likeness of God. This account is simpler and more direct: "Here's your hoe and rake—get to work." This version of creation is pretty much the same as the Sumerian, Akkadian, and

Babylonian versions of creation.

In the Sumerian version, for example, the younger gods and older gods are having family problems—the noisy younger gods give the elder gods a headache. So they create the earth as a kind of getaway—a place where they can party without upsetting the older folks. And when they get there, they create human beings to take care of it for them, like a janitorial staff. Not so different from the second version of creation in the Hebrew Bible.

Meanwhile, back to Genesis.

> And the LORD God commanded the man, "You may freely eat of
> every tree of the garden; but of the tree of the knowledge of good and
> evil you shall not eat, for in the day that you eat of it you shall die."
> (Genesis 2:16–17)

Notice that God doesn't give that command to Eve—she didn't even exist yet in this story. God has some other business to take care of first.

> Then the LORD God said, "It is not good that the man should
> be alone; I will make him a helper as his partner." So out of the
> ground the Lord God formed every animal of the field and every
> bird of the air. (Genesis 2:18–19)

Notice that God doesn't just create woman. He starts out making giraffes and aardvarks and platypuses and warthogs and ducks, "and brought them to the man to see what he would call them; and whatever the man called every living creature, that was its name" (Genesis 2:19).

So God makes a cow, and takes it to Adam, and, playing the good matchmaker, says, "Here, Adam! Just look at her! Isn't she beautiful? Isn't she great? Is she the one?" And Adam says, "Oh, yeah, that's a cow. And yeah, it's a very *nice* cow, God, but I don't know, somehow she just doesn't turn me on." So then God creates a kangaroo, and comes to Adam to see what he'll call her, "Honey-Sweetie-Chickie-Poochie-Pie" or "Maxine," and he says, "Now, this one is *really* special. Isn't she wonderful—what do you think of *her*?" And Adam says, "Oh, yeah, sure, Boss, that's a kangaroo, but . . . well, gee, I'm afraid she's just not my type."

"The man gave names to all cattle, and to the birds of the air, and to every animal of the field; but for the man there was not found a helper as his partner" (Genesis 2:20). This goes on and on through all the animals—none of whom suit Adam. (In this version, God's learning curve appears to be a bit on the steep side, too.)

> So the LORD God caused a deep sleep to fall upon the man, and he
> slept; then he took one of his ribs and closed up its place with flesh.

And the rib that the LORD *God had taken from the man he made
into a woman and brought her to the man. Then the man said,*
"This at last is bone of my bones
and flesh of my flesh;
this one shall be called Woman,
for out of Man this one was taken." (Genesis 2:21–23)

This story is close to Middle Eastern creation myths, too. Among the Babylonians, a war breaks out between the elder and younger gods. The younger gods are led by Marduk, the elder gods by Tiamat (Chaos), who leads an alliance of gods and dwarfs. When Marduk defeats Tiamat, he takes her body and cuts it in half, making the upper half the heavens, and the lower half the earth. He then takes a bone of his defeated enemy—Mummu the Dwarf, as I recall—and encases it in a coating of mud, which he then breathes on to give it life. It becomes the first human being. Sound familiar?

In this version of the story, the blood spilled by the defeated gods has bled into the ground, so the earth that encased the bone has something of the divine in it. It's a fairly insightful picture of the contrary forces that exist in humans, both their earthly nature and their divine aspirations.

At this point in the Genesis story, the man and woman don't yet have names. They're simply the Earthly One and the Living One, and their story is rounded out with a nice little coda: "Therefore a man leaves his father and his mother and clings to his wife, and they become one flesh. And the man and his wife were both naked, and were not ashamed" (Genesis 2:24–25). Considering that the only audience in Eden was all those animals running around in the buff, it's not surprising they weren't.

Anyway, as you see, the version that has Eve being created out of Adam's bone isn't the first one you come across in Genesis: it's just the version that the nine out of ten monks preferred.

THE PLOT THICKENS

Now comes the slithery serpent—another familiar part of the story. But pay attention to what's *not* there.

"Now the serpent was more crafty than any other wild animal that the LORD God had made" (Genesis 3:1). The word "crafty," by the way, just means clever or smart, and in Middle Eastern literature the snake was a symbol of fertility, wisdom, and immortality. None of these attributes are either negative or diabolical. Now look carefully for any reference to the Devil, or to evil. Go ahead. Look for it. You won't find it, because it's not there. It's simply not in the text at all.

So the clever serpent—who apparently is just a serpent—asks Eve a question:

He said to the woman, "Did God say, 'You shall not eat from any tree
in the garden'?" The woman said to the serpent, "We may eat of the
fruit of the trees in the garden; but God said, 'You shall not eat of the
fruit of the tree that is in the middle of the garden, nor shall you
touch it, or you shall die.'" But the serpent said to the woman, "You
will not die. . . ." (Genesis 3:1–4)

And by the way, the serpent is telling the truth. They eat the fruit and they do not die. Gasp! Is God the one who is lying? Because he said to Adam, "of the tree of the knowledge of good and evil you shall not eat, for in the day that you eat of it you shall die" (Genesis 2:17). It's good storytelling. It has impact. It's like the parent saying to the child, "If you're not home by midnight, I'm going to ground you till you're forty-five." Both the parent and the child know that's not literally true, but they both understand that the parent wants to be taken seriously. So does God.

The serpent goes on, "for God knows that when you eat of it your eyes will be opened, and you will be like God, knowing good and evil" (Genesis 3:5). Now note, the serpent does use the word "evil," but look at the context it occurs in. Not "You will *be* evil," but "You will *know* good and evil." You will attain adult discernment.

What is Eve aspiring to here? Knowledge. Is knowledge evil? Of course not. Nowhere do the Scriptures imply that knowledge is evil; knowledge is something we consider good. Knowledge is something human beings seek after—it's the mark of a maturing person. I have to admit, even as a kid I thought Eden would have been dead boring, because I liked learning things. I thought we were given a bad deal here. I still do.

Notice that Eve doesn't take the serpent's word for it, either. She's pretty sharp. She looks at the fruit for herself. "So when the woman saw that the tree was good for food, and that it was a delight to the eyes, and that the tree was to be desired to make one wise" (Genesis 3:6).

Eve is no dummy. The snake knew which of those two to go for. Remember, after all: Adam didn't even know what a helpmeet looked like, but Eve seemed to be on the ball.

She took of its fruit and ate; and she also gave some to her husband,
who was with her, and he ate. Then the eyes of both were opened,
and they knew that they were naked; and they sewed fig leaves
together and made loincloths for themselves. (Genesis 3:6–7)

In other words, suddenly they weren't innocent anymore; they'd begun to understand good and evil. The serpent was right.

Let's think about this as a typical human story for a minute. We all reach that point where we can't really be innocent—or naïve—anymore. Consider the kids I worked with as a counselor in the '60s who'd suddenly become aware of the racial and social injustice in the Norman Rockwell world they lived in. They reacted with guilt, outrage, and often disbelief. Or consider the real shock of the women who suddenly saw the patriarchal mind at work in the churches they loved and trusted. Knowledge may be desirable, but it's also costly.

Like these kids, and like these women, Eve has simply acquired a knowledge that means she'll never again be naïve or innocent. Like us, Eve can never again un-know what she's learned. Paradise and innocence can never be recaptured. But this knowledge is also absolutely imperative for her to grow up to be an independent human being. So Adam and Eve discover they're naked, recognizing a nakedness that's more than simply physical. It's like suddenly being unmasked.

Adam and Eve, then, have been stripped of their innocence, and cannot face themselves, their world—or their creator—with the innocence they had before. This becomes obvious as they face their first encounter with God after their bite of the fatal fruit. Look closely at how it happens.

"They heard the sound of the LORD God walking in the garden at the time of the evening breeze" (Genesis 3:8). (And in case you had any doubts about this version of the story being the work of a second writer, notice that this version of God is not a majestic figure commanding, "Let there be light!" This is a guy in his shirtsleeves, a long day's work behind him, strolling in the back yard before dinner.)

> *And the man and his wife hid themselves from the presence of the LORD God among the trees of the garden. But the LORD God called to the man, and said to him, "Where are you?" He said, "I heard the sound of you in the garden, and I was afraid, because I was naked; and I hid myself." (Genesis 3:8–10)*

This narrative may ring true with many of us. I can remember the point when I became aware of who I was sexually. I was very clear early in my life that I was gay, and that I had to hide it from my family, or I was toast. I knew what it felt like to be unmasked. It was the simultaneous exhilaration of knowledge and the terrifying sense of being stripped naked, of having to hide myself. It might have happened in a different context with some of us. I have a friend who said for her it was the moment she realized that her mother had been having affairs with other men for years, and that she couldn't let her mother—and especially her father—see that knowledge in her. She had to hide it.

"He said, 'Who told you that you were naked? Have you eaten from the tree of which I commanded you not to eat?'" (Genesis 3:11). Now watch this next part very carefully: "The man said, '*The woman whom you gave to be with me*, she gave me fruit from the tree, and I ate'" (Genesis 3:12).

"See, it's *your* fault, God! It isn't my fault! You gave me this woman, and she made me do it." Does this start to sound familiar, either from when you were a kid, or having to deal with kids? "It wasn't my fault! Janie told me to do it!"

Did your mother ever buy that one? Neither did mine. The usual maternal response to that line is: "I see. And if Janie told you to jump off the bridge, would you do that, too?" So what makes us think God will buy it when Adam blames Eve? Do we really think God is dumber than our mothers were?

Notice that God hasn't uttered a word of curse at this point, but humanity has already fallen. The sinister process has already begun. Adam is scapegoating someone else—anyone else. You gave me the woman, he reasons, and the woman gave me the fruit. It's not my fault.

"Then the LORD God said to the woman, 'What is this that you have done?' The woman said, 'The serpent tricked me, and I ate'" (Genesis 3:13). Notice too that the serpent didn't trick Eve. The serpent told her the truth. But Eve joins in the buck-passing. It was the serpent who made her do it, she insists.

Now comes the curse, but observe that the only one who actually gets cursed is the serpent. God doesn't utter a word of curse to Adam and Eve. *And there is still no suggestion that the serpent is anything but a serpent.*

Listen carefully to what God really says:

> *To the woman he said,*
> *"I will greatly increase your pangs in childbearing;*
> *in pain you shall bring forth children,*
> *yet your desire shall be for your husband,*
> *and he shall rule over you." (Genesis 3:16)*

In one sense we can look at this and say, well, yes, this is a text from generations before birth control. You'll get turned on and want to be intimate with this man, and you'll do anything to make him love you, and the next thing you know, you'll be pregnant, and life is going to be a lot harder. It won't just be the two of you anymore. Anyone who has children knows that once you do have a child, you're never free again—not even after they've grown up. Is this a curse—or is it just a description of the way things are when we start to grow up?

And to the man he said,
"Because you have listened to the voice of your wife,
and have eaten of the tree
about which I commanded you,
'You shall not eat of it,'
cursed is the ground because of you;
in toil you shall eat of it all the days of your life;
thorns and thistles it shall bring forth for you;
and you shall eat the plants of the field.
By the sweat of your face
you shall eat bread
until you return to the ground,
for out of it you were taken;
you are dust,
and to dust you shall return." (Genesis 3:17–19)

This is fairly typical of the stories many cultures tell to explain why life can be difficult. The Akkadians, for example, explaining why we have to struggle so hard to grow enough to eat, said that humanity had been created to take care of the earth for the gods. Well, this is a pretty accurate description of the way ancient people had to live life before mechanized agriculture or labor-saving devices. It was one way of explaining quite simply why life was the way it was. Nobody questioned this story as long as life matched the picture it painted. Today, post Industrial Revolution and smack in the middle of the Information Age, people think there's something wrong with having to live by the sweat of your brow. So the story doesn't have the kind of persuasive power it did at one time.

The man named his wife Eve, because she was the mother of all
living. And the LORD God made garments of skins for the man and
for his wife, and clothed them. (Genesis 3:20–21)

Now stop right here and look at this picture of God! God is personally making little coats and skirts and things for Adam and Eve. It's a very different God from the one who says, "Let there be, and there is." This is not God saying, grandly, "Let there be Levis!" No, God is personally sitting down and sewing little clothes out of skins for Adam and Eve. Does this look like a God who suddenly hates humanity? On the contrary. It looks like a God who is still taking care of this man and woman. In the tender image of God as tailor, there's a world of love and caring between creator and creation.

And yet, even God cannot undo what has happened. Adam and Eve are no longer naïve children in the garden, and they can never return to their innocence. How fearsomely this is shown in the scene of the final exit from Eden:

> The LORD God sent him forth from the garden of Eden, to till the
> ground from which he was taken. He drove out the man; and at the
> east of the garden of Eden he placed the cherubim, and a sword
> flaming and turning to guard the way. (Genesis 3:23–24)

IS THERE A LIFE AFTER EDEN?

> Now the man knew his wife Eve, and she conceived and bore Cain,
> saying, "I have produced a man with the help of the LORD." Next she
> bore his brother Abel. (Genesis 4:1–2)

Look carefully at what the text says—and doesn't say. Eve gives the credit to God when she gives birth to her child. She doesn't sound like a woman cursing her lot in life, but a woman praising God for the gift of a son. Now ask yourself this: who is the first person—after God—to create something in the Old Testament? It's Eve, who brings forth a child, proving that she really is in the image and likeness of the creator God. She, at least, recognizes that her ability to create comes from God.

So. Where does it say that Eve is the source of evil, the one who's responsible for all the misery in the world? It's not in the Bible. The text doesn't picture Eve as the incarnation of wickedness but shows us a woman with a perfectly ordinary human curiosity, who both reasons and aspires to knowledge, who has both the power to create, and the grace to credit God with that power. *In fact, the Bible shows us that, despite the exile from Eden, both God and Eve still entertain a great affection for each other.* That's the Eve that the Bible shows us.

We see a woman who seeks growth, who gives thanks for the birth of children, who not only bears children, but lives through the agony of seeing one of them kill the other and be exiled for his crime, and goes right on with life.

"Adam knew his wife again, and she bore a son and named him Seth, for she said, 'God has appointed for me another child instead of Abel, because Cain killed him'" (Genesis 4:25). Even as she grieves her dead child, and she sees her other son sent off into exile, she realizes that life goes on as she gives birth to another son. She'll bear what she has to and get on with loving and raising the new child.

Does this sound like a woman who hates life, or her children, or God? No, this is a woman who still credits God with the gift of her third son. Though she's lost the innocence of Eden, it hasn't killed her, and she's getting on with life. This is a woman who takes life on realistic terms, learning and growing and giving back to life another generation of children to carry life forward. This is emphatically not the Eve of the medieval monks, who really didn't know women or the lives women led, or the Eve of our Sunday School childhoods. That woman isn't really scriptural at all.

The real Eve, it turns out, is a very different person than we've been led to believe. She's not a sinister temptress: you don't find that anywhere in this story. And she's not an ally of the Devil—there's absolutely no hint of that, either.

No, Eve is a woman trying to grow, seeking knowledge, learning to live with the consequences, grieving her child's death and her son's exile, and still retaining a sense of gratitude to God for what she sees God has given her— the ability to create a child. This may not be the Eve of Sunday School, but she's the Eve of the Scriptures—and an Eve I can easily see in the same real-life terms I see women I have actually known.

In fact, our last glimpse of Eve, in Genesis 4:25, shows us a woman rejoicing over the birth of a new child. Despite the regret and the grief, despite the exile from Eden and loss of innocence, she has an unquenchable hope that is reborn with every child she brings into the world, a determination to re-create Eden as the place of safety and care where the newborn can grow. No matter that this child, too, will live beyond innocence one day. Eve and her daughters will continue to mirror God for us: the giver of life whose caring will outlive sin and folly, and whose love will stretch to embrace any number of children. They are both alike in that respect: for Eve is truly the image and likeness of the all-mothering God.

MARIANNE'S STORY

Growing up, I was always fascinated with the story of my however-many-times-great-grandmother, Margaret Cassidy—Peg Cassidy—who came here from Ireland during the Great Famine. When the famine started, she had a husband and four children. Within three years, she'd seen them all die. She wanted to die herself, but somehow she never did. If she hadn't been a good Catholic girl, she might have killed herself, but she knew she couldn't do that. She always said God had something for her to do, so she just kept on living.

One of her neighbors, Michael Cassidy, had lost his wife and all but one of his children, so she went to him and said, "Michael, you've lost all your family and I've lost all mine. Where's the good of staying here and waiting to follow the dead? You need a woman to care for that child and my arms need a child to care for. We're both young enough to make another family if we leave this place." He figured what she said made good sense, and they were married and on a boat for New York within the month.

They had as hard a time staying alive when they first got here as any other Irish immigrant family of the time. There was a lot of prejudice against the Irish, and a growing brood to feed, and not much money to feed them with. Michael worked as a coal-carrier and she worked as a hotel laundress, and pretty soon they had five more children of their own.

Watching people die of hunger back home had done something to Peg, and she could never bear to see a hungry child. No matter how poor they were, most days she brought in at least one or two children from the street to sit down to supper with them.

When the chance offered itself, she took a job working in the hotel kitchen, so she'd be able to take home some of the food that came back from the dining room. It helped feed her own family, and it helped fill many a hungry youngster she brought in from the street.

She and Michael lost three of their children in America, and she may have grieved, but each time she simply reached out and gathered in a homeless waif to fill the empty place. There were plenty of orphans around, and Peg wasn't about to let a child starve for food or for love while she had any to give.

When her own children grew up and left home, she filled their places with more children who needed a family. More than once, somebody simply showed up at her door with a lost, hungry child, and she never turned them away. By the time she died, she'd probably raised thirty children, most of them orphans.

Now, here's a woman I can relate to Eve's story—thrown out into a hard world where it was constant work, giving birth to children only to see them die, but then giving life to more children—whether they were hers or not. All the times she could have shriveled up and died, of sorrow or discouragement, she turned it around by reaching out to somebody else who needed her. She never blamed God for the bad things that happened in her life, whether it was the famine or the death of a child. Every time, she gave thanks to God for another child to love and care for. I only wish I had one-tenth of her love and faith.

In reading the story:

- What doesn't the narrative say that I expect it to say?
- What does the narrative tell me that I don't expect?
- What does the *story* actually tell me about Eve?
- What is her relationship with God at the start of the story?
- Where is she at the end of the story?

Self-reflection and learning:

- Where in my life do I resemble her?
- Have I had an "eye-opening" I can identify in my life?
- What can I learn from her?
- What light does this story throw on my own?

What questions and problems does this still leave unanswered or "in process"?

CHAPTER TWO

Family Values in Abraham, or
"...and Baby Makes Four"

In my family, the women were the storytellers and the children were the listeners. It was a pretty good arrangement. We soaked up the family lore like little sponges from Grandma and Mom, the neighbor lady across the street, and an assortment of aunts. It didn't matter that we'd heard the stories a dozen times; in fact, the more we heard them, the more we loved them. "Oh, come on, tell us the one about Auntie Annuska and the bananas!" And so, sighing greatly, someone would tell us about Auntie Annuska, who'd never seen a banana before she arrived at Ellis Island, where somebody gave her and her younger sister each a box lunch with a banana in it. Well, she was thirteen years old, and in charge of an eleven-year-old sister, and she wanted to look cool and sophisticated, but she just couldn't figure out what she was supposed to do with these things, so she stuck them in her trunk, and they stayed there for four months. So of course we always wanted to hear the story about Auntie Annuska and what happened when they finally opened the trunk. (Auntie Annuska would never eat bananas, by the way.)

Sometimes the stories were tongue in cheek, like the Auntie Annuska story, and sometimes they made you cry, like when you heard the one about how your grandparents sent their two children out of the country to live with Aunt Sadie and Uncle Lou in New York when Hitler came to power, and how they never saw each other again. You heard the stories of how some women came here as picture brides, and some came as widows with small children in tow, and how they had to go to work at whatever they could find to take care of their families.

TEDDY'S STORY

My great-grandmother Hilda came over here some time in the 1880s or '90s. She was thirteen years old, and at that time they didn't let Norwegians land at Ellis Island. They would take them off the ship and put them into boxcars and transport them across the country. At various little towns along the way, the boxcars were opened or dropped off, and the local people bid for the services of the immigrants. It wasn't slavery, but it came pretty close. Well, at thirteen years old, Hilda was already pregnant, and they didn't know who the father was—whether she got pregnant before she left Norway, or got pregnant on the boat, or got pregnant in the boxcar.

She was taken in as a housemaid at the home of a college professor. He had been a drummer with a traveling circus until it folded, and by this time he was a professor of music at Beloit College. She gave birth to my grandfather there, and raised him there. She never married, and this was her only child. To make the story complete, forty years later, her son married her boss's daughter!

They weren't all immigrant stories, either. Some were stories of ordinary lives spent in ordinary places, but lives often lived with quiet courage or rich laughter. These aren't TV sitcom stories. Most of us can look back and say there was someone in our families who was quite a woman, as here:

ELLA'S STORY

My mother was the third person in this country to have open heart surgery, and that was because she badgered the doctor until he was willing to interview her. She literally camped out in his office, because she didn't have enough money for the surgery, but she had two small children to raise, and she knew the surgery was her only chance of living to raise them. So—just like the widow and the unjust judge— she just kept getting into the doctor's face. He'd try to get past her, and she would constantly try to get between him and the door. Finally, he got very huffy and said, "Madam, do you realize I'm a very busy man?"

And my mother's temper got the better of her and she snapped back, "Well, smell me!"

He was so astonished that anyone would address him that way that he said, "I can give you ten minutes." You see, he needed a candidate for this experimental surgery who would simultaneously be an extremely grave case, but have a good chance of survival, and he decided if anyone he had seen had the will to live, it was my mom.

These are the stories I mean—real women in real-life dilemmas. The kinds of stories that Hebrew women told their children and grandchildren and nieces and nephews thousands of years ago. The kinds of stories that eventually found their way into the Bible—like the story of Sarah and Hagar.

Over the millennia, of course, Sarah's story has been distorted in the interests of making Bible-readers into nice, sweet, agreeable little tent keepers. Once we know this, we can't look at the old stories in the same way. So it's important to become aware of the patriarchal agenda in the stories, and the ways in which they distort both the stories and our self-perceptions. But then again, if all we have are the Sunday School pictures of biblical women or a dose of skepticism, we may not bother reading these stories at all. And that would be our loss.

My own experience taught me that there's a kind of a unique strength in some of these stories that reaches me at a very deep level, and it's one of the reasons why I want to break these stories out of *both* the old forms and the new and ask essential questions, like "What or who are these stories *about?*" And when we start looking for the answers, they're not too hard to find. After all, the patriarchs who edited them left us a lot of clues.

We'll see some plain-as-day evidence—and some very strange things—when we look at the story of Sarah and Hagar. Here's a hint: notice how the big patriarch Abraham responds when his wife Sarah tells him to do anything. Instead of looking like the master of the known world, he jumps to whatever she tells him.

THE SAGA BEGINS

The Abraham saga really starts in Genesis 12, 3,700 to 4,000 years ago in the Middle East. There were already some civilizations beginning in that area, large city-states on the Tigris and Euphrates Rivers, the area loosely called Mesopotamia.

The story begins in Ur, a city that was actually excavated in the 1920s by a British archeologist named Sir Leonard Woolley. In the Abraham story, Abraham's father Terah sets out from the city of Ur to go to Haran, northwest of Ur (Genesis 11:27–32).

This doesn't mean they set out and went to Haran as you and I would set out and go to Reno or Chicago. This isn't a world where you get on the freeway and head for your destination. You travel in a group with flocks and herds, with women and kids and old folks walking alongside the animals. It can take years to get from here to there, stopping for the herds to graze or waiting for the weather to change or simply because the group has reached a point of exhaustion. Plus, to show you just how complex this traveling group is, take a look at this:

Abraham[3] and Nahor took wives; the name of Abraham's wife was

Sarah, and the name of Nahor's wife was Milcah. She was the
daughter of Haran the father of Milcah and Iscah. Now Sarah was
barren; she had no child. (Genesis 11:29–30)

These people are more closely related than modern geneticists would be comfortable with—Abraham and Sarah, it turns out, are actually probably half-brother and half-sister. This wasn't unusual: it was a way of keeping the limited wealth in the family. Note also that the only thing we are told about Sarah at this point is that she's barren, which will become the point of tension in the whole story.

Now the LORD said to Abraham, "Go from your country and your
kindred and your father's house to the land that I will show you.
I will make of you a great nation, and I will bless you, and make
your name great, so that you will be a blessing. I will bless those who
bless you, and the one who curses you I will curse; and in you all the
families of the earth shall be blessed." So Abraham went, as the LORD
had told him; and Lot went with him. Abraham was seventy-five
years old when he departed from Haran. (Genesis 12:1–4)

So Abraham takes his wife Sarah and his brother's son, and all the people, sheep, and goats that made up his wealth, and sets out for Canaan. The narrator tosses in the little fact that Abraham is, by this time, seventy-five years old and Sarah was probably just a decade or so younger—a pretty unusual stage to be pulling up stakes and starting over.

AN ODD TAKE ON FAMILY VALUES
But some interesting things start to happen.

Now there was a famine in the land. So Abraham went down to
Egypt to reside there as an alien, for the famine was severe in the
land. When he was about to enter Egypt, he said to his wife Sarah,
"I know well that you are a woman beautiful in appearance; and
when the Egyptians see you, they will say, 'This is his wife'; then they
will kill me, but they will let you live. Say you are my sister, so that it
may go well with me because of you, and that my life may be spared
on your account." (Genesis 12:10–13)

Hmmm. Family values? Not quite the words we'd expect from a proper, God-fearing patriarch! It sounds as if he's perfectly willing to toss his wife to the Egyptians to save his neck. He begins by assuming that some lucky Egyptian will want to snap up the sixty-five-year-old Sarah as a wife.

Note two things here. First of all, Sarah must have been a very impressive woman, at least in Abraham's eyes—not a pretty young girl but a magnificent-looking woman in the way she walked and dressed and acted. She was, after all, the wife of an important man, and Abraham fully expected her to impress the Egyptians.

(A little sideline about "years" in the Old Testament. Age is revered in the Middle Eastern culture—the older you are, the more claim you have to respect. So these stories magnify the age to venerate Abraham and Sarah. "And *our* ancestor was 100 years old." "Well, *our* ancestor was 150!" "And *ours* was 230!" Nobody is really expected to take these years literally—they're just a way of underlining Abraham and Sarah's respectability. Also, it's a terrific way of increasing the tension in the plot, when you start to wonder how a sixty-five-year-old woman is going to be the mother of this great tribe of descendents. Note also, there will be three almost-identical incidents that some scholars call "The Danger to the Ancestress," in which Abraham, and later Isaac, will try to pass his wife off as his sister. The whole story is about ancestry, how one traces oneself back to these people, and how God brings about a promise to prosper Abraham's descendents. So it's terribly important who is the father of Sarah's children. What happens if an Egyptian gets Sarah pregnant and she has a non-Israelite child? What will that do to God's promise?)

A Woman of Stature

Sarah doesn't seem to have any problem with this little deception. Is this because she's so passive? Probably not. Other incidents will show us she's a strong woman who never hesitates to exert her will. Is Abraham's deception—the idea that at sixty-five she is so attractive to other men—flattering to her? Is the thought of being taken into, say, Pharaoh's harem—where she'll probably live a much cushier life than she has in a wandering band—repellent to her? A great many of the women in the royal households weren't necessarily sexual partners for king or pharaoh. The women's quarters in the great temple-cities of the Middle East, for instance, were important economic units that produced fine clothes and embroidery, among other things. This isn't to say that royal harems didn't house sexual partners or child-bearers for the ruler. But the people of Sumer, Akkadia, and Egypt saw the women's houses as places where things with very high market value were produced—the finest carded wool and the finest linen. It's a pattern repeated in the Middle Ages, where the ladies of the court or the ones who surrounded the chatelaine of the castle did fine needlepoint, and so on. Women were economic units, and Sarah doesn't seem upset about this. Indeed, as the wife of a man with a considerable household, Sarah as chief wife wouldn't have been the lowly servant grinding the grain for tonight's bread, but the headwoman directing the others in their tasks and managing the household and its members. She had considerable authority within the household.

Moreover, the story clearly tells us that Abraham has a very high opinion of this woman. He expects people to be envious of him, to find her desirable. If we were in Sarah's place, at sixty-five, we might find that pretty flattering. And the idea of being pampered in a royal household might sound very good after the relative hardship of traveling.

> *When Abraham entered Egypt the Egyptians saw that the woman was very beautiful. When the officials of Pharaoh saw her, they praised her to Pharaoh. And the woman was taken into Pharaoh's house. And for her sake he dealt well with Abraham; and he had sheep, oxen, male donkeys, male and female slaves, female donkeys, and camels. But the LORD afflicted Pharaoh and his house with great plagues because of Sarah, Abraham's wife. (Genesis 12:14–17)*

It looks like God is taking this pretty seriously, and doesn't want Sarah to have an Egyptian child. It also tells us that there's a certain amount of power here—Sarah's presence is powerful enough to be the cause of these plagues coming upon the Egyptians.

> *So Pharaoh called Abraham, and said, "What is this you have done to me? Why did you not tell me that she was your wife? Why did you say, 'She is my sister,' so that I took her for my wife? Now then, here is your wife, take her, and be gone." And Pharaoh gave his men orders concerning him; and they set him on the way, with his wife and all that he had. (Genesis 12:18–20)*

Danger averted, Abraham and Sarah go on their way, their fortunes greatly increased thanks to Sarah.

PROMISES, PROMISES

Presently, lest we forget that Sarah is sixty-five and hasn't yet had a child, God makes another promise:

> *The LORD said to Abraham, after Lot had separated from him, "Raise your eyes now, and look from the place where you are, northward and southward and eastward and westward; for all the land that you see I will give to you and to your offspring forever. I will make your offspring like the dust of the earth; so that if one can count the dust of the earth, your offspring also can be counted. Rise up, walk through the length and the breadth of the land, for I will give it to you."*
> *(Genesis 13:14–17)*

And yet later, God makes a third promise:

> *After these things the word of the LORD came to Abraham in a vision,*
> *"Do not be afraid, Abraham, I am your shield; your reward shall be*
> *very great." But Abraham said, "O Lord GOD, what will you give me,*
> *for I continue childless, and the heir of my house is Eliezer of*
> *Damascus?" And Abraham said, "You have given me no offspring,*
> *and so a slave born in my house is to be my heir." But the word of the*
> *LORD came to him, "This man shall not be your heir; no one but your*
> *very own issue shall be your heir." He brought him outside and said,*
> *"Look toward heaven and count the stars, if you are able to count*
> *them." Then he said to him, "So shall your descendants be." And he*
> *believed the LORD; and the LORD reckoned it to him as righteousness.*
> *(Genesis 15:1–6)*

True, so far, all these promises are being made to Abraham, not Sarah. But the narrator is careful to keep reminding the reader that these promises are dead serious, and that both Abraham and Sarah are getting older and older every time a promise is made. Just how serious the promises are is clearly shown in what follows, one of the most fascinating—and eeriest— passages in the saga.

> *Then he said to him, "I am the LORD who brought you from Ur of the*
> *Chaldeans, to give you this land to possess." But he said, "O LORD*
> *God, how am I to know that I shall possess it?" He said to him,*
> *"Bring me a heifer three years old, a female goat three years old, a*
> *ram three years old, a turtledove, and a young pigeon." He brought*
> *him all these and cut them in two, laying each half over against the*
> *other; but he did not cut the birds in two. And when birds of prey*
> *came down on the carcasses, Abraham drove them away.*
> *(Genesis 15:7–11)*

This is one of the ways you swore a solemn oath in this culture. You split these animals in two, and then you walked between the pieces, in effect saying, "If I break this oath, may I be cut in half as these animals have been cut in half."

And now comes the eerie part:

> *As the sun was going down, a deep sleep fell upon Abraham, and a*
> *deep and terrifying darkness descended upon him. Then the LORD*
> *said to Abraham, "Know this for certain, that your offspring shall be*
> *aliens in a land that is not theirs, and shall be slaves there, and they*
> *shall be oppressed for four hundred years; but I will bring judgment*

on the nation that they serve, and afterward they shall come out with
great possessions. As for yourself, you shall go to your ancestors in
peace; you shall be buried in a good old age. And they shall come
back here in the fourth generation; for the iniquity of the Amorites is
not yet complete."
When the sun had gone down and it was dark, a smoking fire pot
and a flaming torch passed between these pieces. [This is the
presence of God swearing the oath, the covenant.] *On that day the*
Lord made a covenant with Abraham, saying, "To your descendants
I give this land, from the river of Egypt to the great river, the river
Euphrates. . . ." (Genesis 15:12–18)

God has reaffirmed the promise, and affirmed that Abraham's heir will
not be a slave born in his household, but the legitimate heir of his wife, Sarah.
And as for Sarah? The most dramatic part of her story is about to begin, the
contest between Sarah and a young slave woman named Hagar.

THE CONTEST BEGINS

Abraham may be the model of patience as year follows year and decade
follows decade, but Sarah, it appears, isn't quite so content to do nothing.

Now Sarah, Abraham's wife, bore him no children. She had an
Egyptian slave-girl whose name was Hagar, and Sarah said to
Abraham, "You see that the Lord has prevented me from bearing
children; go in to my slave-girl; it may be that I shall obtain children
by her." And Abraham listened to the voice of Sarah. So, after
Abraham had lived ten years in the land of Canaan, Sarah,
Abraham's wife, took Hagar the Egyptian, her slave-girl, and gave her
to her husband Abraham as a wife. He went in to Hagar, and she
conceived; and when she saw that she had conceived, she looked with
contempt on her mistress. (Genesis 16:1–4)

Not exactly Ozzie and Harriet, is it? But it's not as bizarre as it seems. In
the written law codes of ancient cities like Nuzi and Mari in the Middle
East—not far from where our story takes place—if a barren woman had
slaves she could select a slave woman to be her surrogate, to have a child who
would be her legal heir. This is precisely what Sarah is doing. She wants an
heir, and she owns a slave who seems suitable to give birth to an heir for her.

This tells us that Sarah is a woman of wealth and property in her own
right. Slaves, after all, are wealth in this culture, and Hagar is Sarah's property,
not Abraham's, as the law requires. What else does it tell us? For one thing,
God keeps making promises to Abraham, but it doesn't sound as if Sarah is
buying it. She's not just taking her childlessness passively, sitting there like a

sack of damp laundry, feeling sorry for herself. She's a woman determined to cope. "If God isn't coming through with this child," she seems to reason, "there's at least something I can do about this." She's self-confident enough to try nudging God to act a little more quickly. "I have legal remedies and I'm going to take them. Abraham, you and God talk to each other if you like, but I want a son, and by golly, I know how I can make that happen!"

Now, putting yourself in Sarah's place for a moment, consider this. The law gives you a chance to have a child. But the price is that you have to give your husband a woman of child-bearing age who can produce a tolerably intelligent and attractive child. In other words, the surrogate mother must be fairly intelligent and attractive—a big risk for Sarah. She's telling her husband, in effect, "Here's this good looking woman who can have children. Get her pregnant." Abraham's response? "Yes, ma'am."

Though Abraham knows God's promise is to him, he's letting Sarah take matters into her own hand. The power dynamics in the household are summed up in the phrase, "and Abraham listened to the voice of Sarah." Once we take our focus off Abraham as patriarch, and look at his interactions with his wife, we notice something interesting. Abraham always does exactly what Sarah tells him to. There is an almost unspoken "Sure, honey, anything you say," in Abraham's response. Maybe the great patriarch was hen-pecked, but there's something more fundamental behind his willingness to yield to Sarah's demands. In this culture, men do the external business of the family while women are in charge of the household itself, raising the children and acting as the family matchmaker. Abraham doesn't say, "Here's this nice-looking slave I can have a child with." No. It's Sarah who decides which of the slaves is the suitable mother for the child.

So Abraham does as Sarah commands and gets Hagar pregnant.

> When [Hagar] saw that she had conceived, she looked with contempt
> on her mistress. Then Sarah said to Abraham, "May the wrong done
> to me be on you! I gave my slave-girl to your embrace, and when she
> saw that she had conceived, she looked on me with contempt. May
> the LORD judge between you and me!" (Genesis 16:4–5)

Oops! This isn't working out the way Sarah had it planned, and her immediate response is the classic "It's all your fault!" (We'll see later that Sarah tends to disown her actions when they don't bring the desired result.) Abraham's response to Sarah? "Your slave-girl is in your power; do to her as you please." ("Anything you want, honey.") "Then Sarah dealt harshly with her, and she ran away from her" (Genesis 16:6).

Obviously, Abraham doesn't want to get between these two women. Who would?

AND BABY MAKES FOUR

Sarah's plan has gone awry, and Abraham and Hagar take a certain amount of the heat. Hagar, driven to the limits of her endurance, runs away, and returns only after God personally gets into the act (Genesis 16:7–14). Sarah has attempted to force God's hand, but God is still in charge. (This part of the story has some fairly awesome surprises itself, and we'll look at it more closely when we get to Hagar in Chapter 3.) For the moment, things don't look too good for Sarah, and developments in the story paint a less-than-flattering picture of her. This seems not to have bothered the storyteller, who never thought Sarah was a sitcom wife and who hadn't been to Sunday School. Sarah was a real woman, trying to cope and sometimes getting it wrong, and not too happy about it. But the storyteller is undisturbed: life goes on, and presently Baby Ishmael arrives. Interestingly, the story doesn't say anything about how Sarah felt at this juncture. After all, she has an heir. Or does she?

God, as far as we can tell, simply lets this one pass. The child is here. Fine. But as if to underline the fact that Sarah's manipulation wasn't what God had in mind, God reiterates the covenant with Abraham, this time by instituting the rite of circumcision and by changing the names of Abram and Sarai to Abraham and Sarah (Genesis 17:1–15).

> God said to Abraham, "As for Sarah your wife . . . I will bless her, and
> moreover I will give you a son by her. I will bless her, and she shall
> give rise to nations; kings of peoples shall come from her." Then
> Abraham fell on his face and laughed, and said to himself, "Can a
> child be born to a man who is a hundred years old? Can Sarah, who
> is ninety years old, bear a child?" And Abraham said to God, "O that
> Ishmael might live in your sight!" God said, "No, but your wife Sarah
> shall bear you a son, and you shall name him Isaac. I will establish
> my covenant with him as an everlasting covenant for his offspring
> after him. As for Ishmael, I have heard you; I will bless him and
> make him fruitful and exceedingly numerous; he shall be the father of
> twelve princes, and I will make him a great nation. But my covenant
> I will establish with Isaac, whom Sarah shall bear to you at this
> season next year." (Genesis 17:15–21)

Notice that over and over again, God makes promises, but no child is born. They go into Egypt, God rescues Sarah—but no child is born. God makes another promise—but no child is born. Hagar gets pregnant and has a son, but for Sarah, in effect, still no child. Everybody's getting older and older, and the narrator makes sure you know just exactly how much older.

There's something moving in Abraham's plea for the son born to him and Hagar. After all, he loves the child regardless of who the mother is. But

God remains unmoved. Ishmael will be well cared for; he will not be forgotten. But the son Sarah contrived to have born isn't the son who was intended. Period.

WHY DID SARAH LAUGH?

This brings us to one of the most wonderful passages in the story: Abraham, relaxing in the door of his tent in the heat of the day, is visited by three strangers, whom he greets with true Middle Eastern hospitality, insisting that they rest themselves while he has a feast prepared for them (Genesis 18:1–8).

The hearers of the Old Testament assumed that the strangers were three angels sent by God; the early Christians interpreted the three strangers as the Trinity. Whatever the interpretation, it's clear that something momentous is happening under the oaks at Mamre. For the strangers not only sit down to eat, but the following exchange takes place.

> They said to him, "Where is your wife Sarah?" And he said, "There, in the tent." Then one said, "I will surely return to you in due season, and your wife Sarah shall have a son." And Sarah was listening at the tent entrance behind him. Now Abraham and Sarah were old, advanced in age; it had ceased to be with Sarah after the manner of women. So Sarah laughed to herself, saying, "After I have grown old, and my husband is old, shall I have pleasure?" (Genesis 18:9–12)

What a delicious picture of Sarah, listening in her tent, practically rolling on the floor at the thought of having a child at this late date. Maybe her words are simply the bitter sarcasm of a woman who knows she'll never have a child.

> The LORD said to Abraham, "Why did Sarah laugh, and say, 'Shall I indeed bear a child, now that I am old?' Is anything too wonderful for the LORD? At the set time I will return to you, in due season, and Sarah shall have a son." But Sarah denied, saying, "I did not laugh"; for she was afraid. He said, "Oh yes, you did laugh."
> (Genesis 18:13–15)

Sarah herself suddenly seems to tumble to the fact that there might be something more here than a group of ordinary travelers stopping for lunch. Notice that just as she disowned her responsibility for Hagar's pregnancy, she disowns her own reactions now. "I didn't laugh!" she insists. But God has heard the laughter, and Sarah herself will remember it eventually, however much she denies it now.

Having delivered yet one more promise—this time, at long last, in Sarah's hearing—the three strangers go on their way, to pay a visit to Sodom and Gomorrah, a little novella (Genesis 18:20–19:38) in which Abraham comically bargains with God over the fate of a famously sinful city. It provides a reminder that the people who originally told and wrote down the Scriptures knew perfectly well this passage was supposed to have an element of humor in it. After all, they didn't know they were writing Scriptures—they thought they were just telling stories. Remember this when you consider the story of Sarah. Centuries before anybody regarded this tale as sacred writ, it was just a *story*, and if we're to understand it today, we must approach it as exactly that.

In any event, the narrator, with true narrative skill, leaves the story of Sarah hanging and takes us on a little trip through the destruction of Sodom and Gomorrah, Lot's wife being turned into a pillar of salt, and his daughters getting him drunk and tricking him into getting them pregnant. (We'll say nothing of family values here.) At last the narrator takes us back to the Abraham-and-Sarah narrative thread just in time for the second danger scene, which plays out very much like the danger the couple faced back in Egypt.

THE SECOND DANGER (GENESIS 20)

This time Abraham and his family go to Abimelech, the King of Gerar. Again, Abraham tells the people of Gerar that Sarah is his sister. Keep in mind that by this time he's over ninety, and she's well over eighty, and he's still afraid that the King of Gerar will think Sarah's so attractive he'll kill Abraham to get her. Again, Sarah, impressive as ever, is taken into the king's harem, but God, not about to have a Canaanite inherit the promise, makes all the women in Gerar—and even all the animals—become barren. *Nobody* can have any children while Sarah is in the king's harem. God, however, seems to have a certain sympathy for King Abimelech, telling him in a dream who Sarah really is, and assuring him that God regards him as blameless, "It was I," God says to Abimelech, "who kept you from sinning."

Abimelech, understandably upset, complains to Abraham, who, relenting, removes the curse from the people of Gerar, and makes out even better than he did in Egypt. Abimelech not only hands over Sarah as quickly as he can, but throws in some sheep, some goats, and a thousand pieces of silver. Anything, he seems to say—just get this guy and his wife out of here. Interestingly enough, he's charming to Sarah. "Look, [he says] I have given your brother a thousand pieces of silver; it is your exoneration before all who are with you; you are completely vindicated" (Genesis 20:16). This done, God makes Abimelech and the people of Gerar fertile again.

SARAH LAUGHS AT LAST

As the wombs of all the women in Gerar open up again, Sarah's womb, too, is quickened. The long-awaited event finally comes to pass.

> *The LORD dealt with Sarah as he had said, and the LORD did for*
> *Sarah as he had promised. Sarah conceived and bore Abraham a son*
> *in his old age, at the time of which God had spoken to him. Abraham*
> *gave the name Isaac to his son whom Sarah bore him.*
> *(Genesis 21:1–3)*

The elderly couple names their baby Isaac: "Laughter," a lovely response to Sarah's long-awaited gift: "Now Sarah said, 'God has brought laughter for me; everyone who hears will laugh with me.'" (Genesis 21:6)

Obviously, she too is remembering the moment when she sat in her tent, laughing incredulously at the angelic visitors. She denied her laughter then, but God has fulfilled it all the same. Despite her incredulity and her attempts to force God's hand, God responds with generosity and Sarah responds with gratitude, affirming that God has not only given her laughter, but that everyone else will share that laughter, too.

Or *almost* everybody.

Remember the little problem of that extra son, Ishmael—the one who was supposed to be Sarah's heir, but is in fact Hagar's son?

> *The child grew, and was weaned; and Abraham made a great feast*
> *on the day that Isaac was weaned. But Sarah saw the son of Hagar*
> *the Egyptian, whom she had borne to Abraham, playing with her son*
> *Isaac. So she said to Abraham, "Cast out this slave woman with her*
> *son; for the son of this slave woman shall not inherit along with my*
> *son Isaac." (Genesis 21:8–10)*

Legally, of course, Ishmael was born to be Sarah's son, but now Sarah repudiates her own agreement. From this point on in the story, Sarah refers to Ishmael only as "the son of the slave woman," or "her son." This is real disownment, and it makes her earlier moments of disownment look mild. She's already disowned her part in Hagar's pregnancy (Genesis 16:5) and her laughter in the tent (Genesis 18:15). But now, in a very painful scene, she disowns the very child who was born only because she insisted on it. Up until this point, Ishmael was Sarah's legal heir. but now that she has a son of her own, the deal is off. Get rid of this woman and *her* son.

This isn't a pretty picture of Sarah, but it's probably an honest one. We may not admire it, but it rings all too true to life. She's waited nearly a century—a hundred years!—for her son to be born, and she's fiercely protective of him and his future. She can't bear the sight of the rival heir, or the woman who gave birth to him. Rather than turn our backs on this less-than-perfect picture of Sarah, we should instead grieve for our sister, who still couldn't trust God, even in the midst of her good fortune. This is Sarah: a woman who never fully trusts others, who tries to manipulate people and events, and who discovers that each time she does, life becomes more complicated. And in this case, more sad and unjust.

> *The matter was very distressing to Abraham on account of his son.*
> *But God said to Abraham, "Do not be distressed because of the boy*
> *and because of your slave woman; whatever Sarah says to you, do as*
> *she tells you, for it is through Isaac that offspring shall be named for*
> *you. As for the son of the slave woman, I will make a nation of him*
> *also, because he is your offspring." So Abraham rose early in the*
> *morning, and took bread and a skin of water, and gave it to Hagar,*
> *putting it on her shoulder, along with the child, and sent her away.*
> *And she departed, and wandered about in the wilderness of*
> *Beer-sheba. (Genesis 21:11–14)*

At this point, Hagar goes off to her own encounter with God, and Sarah more or less fades into the background until her death. She's lived long enough to see God's promise brought to pass, she's borne the promised son; the rest is with God. The Bible doesn't tell us Sarah's reaction to the famous story of Isaac's sacrifice (Genesis 22:1–19), in which God commands Abraham to sacrifice Isaac as a burnt offering, only to relent at the last minute and substitute a ram. I've always assumed Sarah knew nothing of this until it was over with. Given her ferocity on her son's behalf, and her tendency to trust in her own abilities rather than God's promises, it's unlikely she would have risked her boy this way. But she did live to see Isaac grown to manhood—she reached the ripe old age of 127, about thirty-seven years after Isaac was born.

After her death, Abraham marries a woman named Keturah, and has a huge number of sons by her. But he "gave all he had to Isaac. But to the sons of his concubines Abraham gave gifts, while he was still living, and he sent them away from his son Isaac, eastward to the east country" (Genesis 25:5–6). Sarah's son will be the unrivalled heir of Abraham's line, exactly as God (and Sarah herself) wished.

WHO WAS THIS WOMAN?

Once her story is complete, we're left with many questions. It's a remarkable story, and it's impossible to see Sarah as anything other than a remarkable woman. Consider some of what we've seen: Sarah is a woman of property and presence, probably beautiful and impressive, too. She's clearly the headwoman, who tells all the other women in the band what to do. She's the one who decides who'll tend the band's numerous children, who'll spin the wool, who'll tend to the elderly or frail, who'll oversee the lesser servants who prepare the food. She occupies a position of power, and she knows what and where her powers are. Abraham may make the treaties and deal with the outsiders—that's what men do in this culture. But Sarah's place—and power—is at the heart of the family.

What do we know about her personality? She can be jealous, even fiercely so. She isn't someone you'd care to cross. And she's certainly not a passive person who does not try to shape life to her own ends. Consider her relationship with God. When we hear the Abraham story read in church or Sunday School, he's extolled as a model of virtue and faith, as in "the LORD reckoned it to [Abraham] as righteousness" (Genesis 15:6). Abraham, after all, took God's word for it, and trusted God that it would come about.

Sarah, on the other hand, seems to be riddled with doubts and misgivings. There's a good deal of subtle humor in the picture of Sarah nudging God a little, especially when you consider that whenever she took things in her own hands, they got more complicated. There's something irresistibly human in Sarah, thinking how simple it looks, saying, "Here, take my slave girl, and let her have a child for me." Unfortunately for Sarah, Hagar is a real person, too, and when she finds out she's pregnant, she feels she has an advantage over her mistress. Like most of us, Sarah discovers that plans that look good on paper sometimes go horribly wrong.

True, Sarah really does have a problem: she lives in a culture in which, if she doesn't have a son, she'll be a powerless dependent for the rest of her life if she becomes widowed. It's a culture in which no one can survive alone—everyone, especially the wandering herders and traders, lives in tribes and bands. When all your security depends on the band, one of the most important things is what governs your relationship with the other people within that band. (As an aside, this is why, in the Ten Commandments, only three of the Commandments actually have anything to do with God. Most of them, in fact, are about how you are to live with other people.)

Here is the tragedy of people caught in this culture: Hagar, a slave, is essentially helpless, while Sarah, a powerful woman in her own way, is still—as a woman without a son—potentially just as helpless as Hagar. Each of the women, in different ways, is just trying to survive.

Abraham, on the other hand, can afford to have a different kind of relationship with God. He's quite respectful, and in some ways, even passive, agreeing to whatever God demands. Sarah's relationship with God is more adversarial. She's a good woman who does everything she's supposed to do—except fulfill her primary obligation of producing a son. In the eyes of her culture, it's God who's denied her a son for some reason, but there was always a suspicion that it was somehow the woman's fault. Yes, that would certainly produce a lot more emotional tension in Sarah's relationship with God.

Let's peek into the tent again as Sarah listens to the conversation between the visitors and Abraham, and notice some interesting points. Sarah is eavesdropping. There may be more than a little sarcasm in her laughter.

"Yeah, right, tell me another one!" But as soon as she realizes that her laughter's been overheard, she becomes terrified and denies it. There's a hiddenness in Sarah, a hint that she's a far more complex person than Abraham.

Abraham, after all, can afford to be trusting in a way that Sarah can't. God gives Abraham all kinds of assurances, personal conversations, and covenants, while gets all her information second-hand. She's left to her own resources, and it's small wonder she feels the need to go ahead and do something to bring about her own dreams, even though it means taking some very big risks. Her scope of action may seem more restricted than Abraham's, but she uses it to its fullest extent, with ingenuity and courage.

Even when Sarah is taken into Pharaoh's house, or the harem of King Abimelech, she proves herself to be somebody very much in command of herself rather than a passive victim. (Of course, as the headwoman in Abraham's band, she'd expect to be in charge of the women in Pharaoh's or Abimelech's household, too.) Moreover, look at what happens when Sarah is put in this position of danger. Pharaoh's household is beset with plagues; Abimelech's household is stricken with barrenness. There's power at work here, and Sarah is at the center of it. In the Old Testament mindset, the closer something is to the center of holiness, the more dangerous its position is.

Sarah: Power and Holiness

Holiness equals danger in the Old Testament mind. In a remarkable book called *Purity and Danger*, British anthropologist Mary Douglas explores this in ways that throw light on Sarah's story.[4] Briefly, the closer you are the Holy of Holies (the enclosed area at the very center of the Temple where the Ark of the Covenant sits, with the Spirit of God enthroned upon it), the greater the danger. In the temple, only the High Priest can enter the Holy of Holies. The priests and Levites could enter the area just outside it. The ordinary Israelites could enter the area outside that one. And women could come in only as far as the Court of the Women. Gentiles couldn't enter the Temple proper at all. To go closer to the center of the holy than you're allowed to is to pollute the Temple itself. And the closer you are the center of the holy, the deadlier the pollution.

In the Old Testament world, there's always a certain fear of woman's power, especially the process of giving life, the process of childbirth. Birth is celebrated, deeply desired—and because it borders on a holy mystery, it's essentially dangerous and polluting. To come too close is to become unclean. In the Old Testament, the issue of clean and unclean is paramount. A thing is clean if it's where it belongs. It's unclean if it's outside where it belongs. Blood is used as a cleansing agent to sprinkle on the people to cleanse them from their sins. But if blood isn't properly contained—as in a running sore, or a menstruating or childbearing woman—it's unclean and it can pollute you.

Sarah has been chosen to give birth to the promised heir, which underlines how important she is to the story, and her sexual nature is a danger for both the Egyptians and the people of Gerar. She's both powerful and holy.

Her power isn't simply subjective, either: she's the one who tells Abraham to get her servant girl pregnant, and later orders him to send Hagar and Ishmael away. She fully expects that he'll do as she tells him. These aren't the actions we'd expect of a 1950s suburban housewife, but of a woman who understands the nature of the power she wields.

And what of Sarah as a woman of God? Though she gradually comes to a different understanding of God, it's a long, slow process altogether. She takes things into her own hands; she pushes the envelope. But she also knows when she's gone too far. True, she remains a woman of her culture who doesn't hesitate to have her son's rival sent away. (In fairness to her, Ishmael is fifteen at Isaac's birth, an adult male who'll be an active danger to Sarah's infant son, should Abraham die.) And yet, she shows her softer, more tender side after Isaac's birth, when she says, "God has made me laugh, and everyone will laugh with me."

For Sarah, it's been a long, hard journey to that moment of laughter, but at least for a moment she knows she's been blessed, and she invites all who hear her story to laugh with her. Imperfect? Oh, yes. But strong and unafraid to take a risk for what she desires? Oh, yes again.

Sarah is one of God's truly unforgettable women, and a woman whose heirs and heiresses are found in many stories today. In fact, Sarah herself lives inside most of us—especially those of us who really want to trust God, but haven't always got the patience or the faith to. Like Sarah, we too long for the moment when God's promise will come true. But like Sarah, we too may have to walk a long and difficult way before we find ourselves overwhelmed and finally convinced by the laughter of God.

DOROTHY'S STORY

You want a story? I got one. My great-aunt—Auntie Anna—was an honest-to-God picture bride. That's right. She left Naples just before World War I to come over here and marry a guy she'd never even met. And it's not as if she couldn't find a husband there at home, either. This was a really good-looking woman, lots of personality, always a live wire. I know, I've seen the pictures. She could have married half-a-dozen guys, according to her sister. But I think she wanted more than she could have had staying at home in Naples, and she wasn't afraid to take a chance or two. I don't know, maybe she was just plain adventurous.

In those days, you know, there were a lot of single men who came over from Italy to the States to work, because there were jobs here, but not a lot of single women came over. And when it came time to find a wife, of course all these Italian guys wanted to marry a nice Italian girl from their home town, but of course, there just weren't that many here. That's how a lot of these picture marriages happened. Fortunately for everybody, Italians tend to have big families, which means everybody had a sister or a niece or something back home, so matches could be made pretty often.

Auntie Anna's brothers were already in the States, working in the steel mills in Pittsburgh, and they had a couple of paisans—buddies they worked with—who were looking for wives. So they sent their friends' pictures back home for their sisters to look at. Well, Auntie Anna was eighteen and her sister Livia was seventeen, so because Auntie Anna was the older one, she got the first pick of the two men.

Well, one of the guys who had sent a picture was very handsome, a real heart-throb, looked like a regular movie star. But the other one—she always said he looked like somebody'd hit him in the face with a door, he was so homely. And you know what Auntie Anna did? This good-looking live wire? She picked the homely guy! No kidding. Really. She figured that the good-looking one probably thought too well of himself, so he'd be too hard to please. But the homely guy? He'd probably be so grateful to any woman who'd want to marry him that he'd be really easy to get along with.

She was pretty smart for somebody who was only eighteen, because it turned out she was absolutely right! My Uncle Joe thought she fell right out of the sky, that she was the smartest, prettiest, best woman on earth. Nothing was too good for her. If you asked him about something—anything—he'd just laugh and say, "Ask my wife. She's the brains in this family." He brought home his paycheck, turned it over to her, and let her make the decisions. Whatever Auntie Anna decided was best for the family, Uncle Joe backed her one hundred percent. Didn't matter what it was. Whatever Auntie Anna wanted, Uncle Joe did his best to get it.

He never really worried about anything, either. He used to say, "She does the praying in this family. I just go along to church for the ride. God isn't going to listen to a mug like me, anyway, but how can he turn Anna down? You wait, you'll see. It'll be all right." And it always was. I guess he figured God just had to love Auntie Anna as much as he did.

Isn't that some story? They were really an unusual couple for that time, too. It sure wasn't like that with most families in my neighborhood, that a man would think that much of his wife's opinions or her brains! I get the feeling it might have been like that for Abraham, too, though. It looks like he knew he had a wife who was *beautiful and smart and he expected everyone to envy him. I mean, here's this guy who expects everybody to want his eighty-year-old wife. We should all be so lucky! Sure, he let Sarah call the shots, deciding which of the servants could give him a son, and when it was time to make sure her own son got his inheritance. Obviously, he trusted her. He backed her one hundred percent, just like Uncle Joe backed Auntie Anna. They both knew they were married to very special women.*

And they were special! Women like Auntie Anna and Sarah were realists, first of all. They certainly didn't expect life to be perfect, and they knew you had to take some risks to make it better than it was. Like, Auntie Anna came to a strange country to marry a man she'd never met, and Sarah gave her husband another woman in order to have a son. Would I do such a thing? Would most women? That's pretty gutsy, when you think about it. Sarah must have felt she could trust Abraham as much as he trusted her, which says a lot about their marriage.

When you come down to it, I think Sarah and Auntie Anna would have liked each other, but I bet Abraham and Uncle Joe would have disagreed about whose wife was the smartest and the most beautiful.

QUESTIONS FOR STUDY AND REFLECTION

In reading the story:
- What does the narrative tell us about this woman? Her position? Problems and desires? Personality?
- What makes her tick?
- What strengths does she have? What flaws?
- What is her relationship with God like?
- Where is she at the end of the story?

Self-reflection and learning:
- Where in my life do I resemble her?
- How have I dealt with problems in ways similar to hers?
- What can I learn from her, either good or bad?
- Has someone else played "Sarah" in my life?

What questions and problems does this still leave unanswered or "in process"?

CHAPTER THREE

"The Mother of All Believers":
Hagar's Journey to Freedom

"ALL MY CHILDREN," GENESIS-STYLE

By now, it may be clear that family values in the Old Testament aren't exactly what we thought they were. The family of Abraham, Sarah, and Hagar was custom-made for daytime TV. If they couldn't have found a living on one of the better soaps, they'd have been dynamite on the talk shows. Picture Dr. Phil learning forward and asking, "Tell me, Sarah, how did you feel when you found out that Hagar was pregnant by your husband?" Although the more intriguing question might be, "Tell me, Hagar, how did you feel when you managed to get pregnant before your mistress did?"

It's interesting that nobody really thinks of asking Hagar, but at first she seems to be just a token moved about the board by Sarah, her mistress. But as we unfold this story, we'll see some surprises we probably aren't expecting. Hagar's part in the story is quite small compared to Abraham's or Sarah's, but if we read carefully, it's clear that at one time it was a much bigger role. Later storytellers, for reasons not obvious to modern readers, edited parts of the story out.

Note at the very outset that Hagar may have a bit part in the Hebrew Bible, but in Islam, she plays a starring role. She's the Mother of All Believers, the woman whose story is so central to Islam that it's re-enacted in the pilgrimage to Mecca. (That's right: the pilgrimage to Mecca re-enacts Hagar's journey, not Abraham's.)

This is just part of the odd tension that lives at the heart of the story, a story that appears and re-appears with tantalizing irregularity in Genesis, and just as mysteriously disappears again, only to surface later with the merest hint that something is missing. Something, it seems, has been cut from the text.

I say this simply as a warning for what's to follow. This story is a bit different than the other ones we'll examine. For one thing, we'll look at more than just the biblical source. To tell Hagar's story fairly, we must also look to the tradition of those who trace their journey back to her—the Islamic retelling of her story. In some places, the two versions will agree. In others, they'll tell two very different tales.

By looking at both, we'll see a more three-dimensional portrait of Hagar as she really is, a woman who begins as a slave and ends up as a woman of power, status, and respect, a woman whose story will take us from slavery to freedom, from hopelessness to faith.

Hagar's story is told in just two passages in Genesis, 16:1–16 and 21:8–22—a brief tale compared to the Sarah-Abraham thread, and interrupted by several other narrative incidents. It contains at least one glaring inconsistency (Ishmael's age in 21:15–16, where he regresses from a fifteen-year-old young man to a baby in arms in the space of a few verses), all of which leaves the impression that nobody was paying a lot of attention.

But hidden in these brief passages are some powerful themes that show a face of God we haven't yet seen. God speaks as a friend to Abraham, keeps distant from Sarah, and—amazingly—shows a very different face to the "unimportant" slave girl.

Abraham's God is the God of the covenant; Sarah's is the one who withholds the son from her womb. For Hagar, God is a God of vision, who sees and who gives—or withholds—sight to others.

When we first see Hagar, she is a mere appendage to Sarah's story.

> *Now Sarah, Abraham's wife, bore him no children. She had an*
> *Egyptian slave-girl whose name was Hagar, and Sarah said to*
> *Abraham, "You see that the LORD has prevented me from bearing*
> *children; go in to my slave-girl; it may be that I shall obtain children*
> *by her." And Abraham listened to the voice of Sarah. So, after*
> *Abraham had lived ten years in the land of Canaan, Sarah,*
> *Abraham's wife, took Hagar the Egyptian, her slave-girl, and gave her*
> *to her husband Abraham as a wife. He went in to Hagar, and she*
> *conceived; and when she saw that she had conceived, she looked with*
> *contempt on her mistress. (Genesis 16:1–4)*

As we saw earlier, this was a practice recognized by law, which allowed a woman to designate a slave woman to be a surrogate, to bear a child who would be the woman's heir. But there's an interesting little tidbit here. In the original Hebrew, Sarah says, referring to Hagar, "Perhaps I may be built up from her" (Genesis 16:2).

Sarah's attempts to hurry God's actions, of course, don't work out the way she intends and her plan to be "built up" backfires. Hagar sees that she has conceived, which her mistress has been unable to do, and she immediately looks with contempt on Sarah. Far from being "built up," Sarah is looked down upon by her inferior! (Or to put it another way, Hagar isn't only a bit smug about the fact that she has gotten pregnant—she's downright uppity about it.)

HAGAR'S RISE BEGINS

Hagar's position has actually risen considerably because of her pregnancy. She's now either a minor official wife or concubine (the text isn't quite clear about this)—but more important, she's going to bear her mistress's heir.

This isn't what Sarah had in mind, and as usual, she's not exactly gracious about admitting she's made a mistake.

> *Then Sarah said to Abraham, "May the wrong done to me be on you!*
> *I gave my slave-girl to your embrace, and when she saw that she had*
> *conceived, she looked on me with contempt. May the LORD judge*
> *between you and me!" But Abraham said to Sarah, "Your slave-girl*
> *is in your power; do to her as you please." Then Sarah dealt harshly*
> *with her, and she [Hagar] ran away from her. (Genesis 16:5–6)*

Sarah has a tendency to disown her acts when they don't work out as planned, and here she's at her most characteristic. "My injury be on you!" In other words, "It's all your fault!" It isn't difficult to read in this her underlying anguish and sense of failure. Yes, legally she can have an heir, but probably that's not really what she wants. She wants a son, and Hagar has achieved what she's been denied.

Abraham prudently decides to stay out of Sarah's way. "See, your maid servant is in your hands. Do to her what is good in your eyes." Again, it's the famous Abrahamic phrase "Whatever you say, honey." And what was good in Sarah's eyes was so far from good that Hagar felt forced to run away.

THE MEETING AT THE WELL

The next scene is one of the most astonishing in all the Old Testament, once you know what to look for. It's a meeting at a well. And for those who originally heard this story, a meeting at a well had special significance.[5]

Meetings at wells occur several times in the Old Testament, and each time the encounter is associated with a hero's journey and his ultimate destiny. Generally, the hero flees from trouble in his native land and at a well meets the woman who'll become his betrothed and the mother of his children. There's Jacob's meeting with Rachel (Genesis 29:1–12) and Moses' encounter with the daughters of Reuel (Jethro) (Exodus 2:15–21). There are other variations, too: the betrothal of Isaac and Rebekah, where the servant sent to find a wife for

his master's son encounters the young Rebekah at a well (Genesis 24:11–25).
And there's the truly astonishing meeting of Jesus and the Samaritan woman
at the well, where Jesus reveals his identity for the first time.

But this meeting is different. To begin with, Hagar isn't a hero—she's not
a Moses or a Jacob. She's an abused slave-girl, a foreigner, who isn't looking
for a betrothal and wedding—she's already pregnant! But at the well she has
a meeting with destiny, for she encounters not the betrothed, but the presence
of God, in the form of the angel. And sometimes, in the Old Testament, an
angel isn't just God's messenger, but God.

On the surface it's a simple enough scene:

> The angel of the LORD found her by a spring of water in the
> wilderness, the spring on the way to Shur. And he said, "Hagar, slave-
> girl of Sarah, where have you come from and where are you going?"
> She said, "I am running away from my mistress Sarah."
> (Genesis 16:7–8)

The angel's first words place Hagar and her situation clearly before us.
She is "Hagar, slave-girl of Sarah"; her destiny is not, after all, in her own
hands. Her entire identity is "the slave-girl of Sarah," in whose power she is.
Sarah had handed her over to Abraham; Abraham has handed her back over
to Sarah. To the angel's question "Where have you come from and where are
you going?" she can only reply, "I am running away from my mistress Sarah,"
answering only the first question. Obviously, she doesn't know the answer to
the second.

The angel, however, *does* know the answer, and now tells it to Hagar:

> The angel of the LORD said to her, "Return to your mistress, and
> submit to her." The angel of the LORD also said to her, "I will so
> greatly multiply your offspring that they cannot be counted for
> multitude."
> And the angel of the LORD said to her,
> "Now you have conceived and shall bear a son;
> you shall call him Ishmael,
> for the LORD has given heed to your affliction.
> He shall be a wild ass of a man,
> with his hand against everyone,
> and everyone's hand against him;
> and he shall live at odds with all his kin." (Genesis 16:9–12)

How far the distance is between Sarah's vision of the future and God's!
The angel's command to return to her mistress isn't simply a command to
return to slavery. No, God now reveals that Hagar herself has a special destiny,

and gives her a promise almost identical to the one given to Abraham. Her offspring will become a multitude, for God has seen her affliction. Moreover, God reveals the child's destiny, which may sound odd to us: "the child will be a wild ass of a man, with his hand against everyone, and everyone's hand against him."

If offspring of extraordinary virtue are promised to the righteous, it seems fitting, somehow, that the defenseless slave-girl, mistreated by her mistress, is promised a son who will "strike back." Certainly nothing in the passage that follows suggests that Hagar is the least dismayed by the picture. She responds with words of wonder and joy:

> So she named the LORD who spoke to her, "You are El-roi"; for she
> said, "Have I really seen God and remained alive after seeing him?"
> Therefore the well was called Beer-lahai-roi [the Well of the Living
> One who sees me]. It lies between Kadesh and Bered.
> (Genesis 16:13–14)

God's ironic answer to Sarah's desire to be built up is that Hagar, the "nobody," isn't just promised that she'll be the mother of a son, but that she'll be the ancestress of a multitude. The slave girl is given status far beyond Sarah's. God has given her the vision that Sarah will be less important than her mistreated servant.

A WOMAN APART

There's something extraordinary in this scene that we may not recognize at first. There are only two women in the entire Old Testament who have a direct vision or encounter with God, and to whom a divine annunciation of a promised child of destiny is given. Hagar is the first of them. (The other woman isn't even given a name; she's merely "the wife of Manoah," who becomes the mother of Samson [Judges 13:2–25]. Even Hannah, the mother of Samuel, receives only second-hand assurance—from Eli, the priest—that God will hear her prayer for a son.)

Clearly, Hagar is a woman apart, and the picture of God we're shown here is extraordinary. Its original hearers would probably not expect such an event to occur to any woman, much less a mere servant. But this is the God who sees the affliction of the powerless, and who has the power to overturn or set aside the best of human efforts or expectations. No matter how cleverly Sarah plans things, God will have the heir who was promised, not the one arranged for by Sarah. But God will still bless Abraham's "extra" offspring.

Hagar not only proclaims the reality of her encounter with God ("the living one who sees me"), but she does something even more extraordinary: *she names a well.* As far as I know, she's the only woman in the Old Testament who does, and it's a clue that clearly sets Hagar apart. Women name children;

men name wells. Why? Because to name a well is to establish a right to it. It's a property claim of sorts, a way of saying that Hagar now has the right to draw water from this well. (We'll see the significance of this later.)

We've already got a picture of Hagar at complete odds with the usual women in the Old Testament. Singled out by God, she can claim for herself the well where the meeting took place. Hagar knows where her power comes from: it comes from God, and God alone.

Immediately after naming the well, the storyteller goes on, "Hagar bore Abraham a son; and Abraham named his son, whom Hagar bore, Ishmael" (Genesis 16:15). In other words, God acts immediately to fulfill the promise to Hagar. The son is born. Oddly enough, the lines say, "Hagar bore Abraham a son," not "Hagar bore a son for Sarah," as per the original plan. Why are we not surprised?

Later in the story, when Sarah still hasn't received her promised son, Abraham pleads for Ishmael, saying "O that Ishmael might live in your sight!" (Genesis 17:18). Though God still insists that the covenant will be made with Isaac, he says: "As for Ishmael, I have heard you; I will bless him and make him fruitful and exceedingly numerous; he shall be the father of twelve princes, and I will make him a great nation" (Genesis 17:20). Even Sarah's offspring don't rank as princes! The slave-girl will indeed be the mother of a proud heritage.

THE OUTCASTS

Sarah, of course, has her promised son at long last, but her ecstatic laughter doesn't mean that all will now be well. In the midst of the great feast celebrating the weaning of Isaac,

> Sarah saw the son of Hagar the Egyptian, whom she had borne to Abraham, playing with her son Isaac. So she said to Abraham, "Cast out this slave woman with her son; for the son of this slave woman shall not inherit along with my son Isaac." (Genesis 21:9–10)

So much for Sarah's legal maneuver to have an heir. She's just repudiated the bargain. The son who was to be her heir is now "the son of this slave woman," who won't inherit with "my son Isaac." Needless to say, this upsets Abraham, but God reassures him that he will indeed make a great nation of Ishmael (Genesis 21:12–13).

Abraham reluctantly sends Hagar and Ishmael away. He places food, water, and *the child* on Hagar's shoulder. The boy who was circumcised at thirteen, two years earlier, has suddenly reverted from the age of fifteen to infancy. (And fifteen in this culture is marriageable age: Ishmael is an adult.) True, it makes a more dramatic story, but is that the only reason the storyteller let this blunder get by?

Clearly, the storyteller sees Hagar as the only adult—the only active agent—in the following scene. Hagar encountered the messenger of God at the well, where the destiny of the child was revealed to her. Now, entering the wilderness a second time, she encounters God again. Even with an adult male at hand, it is Hagar's encounter, a continuation of her earlier meeting with God.

Hagar is again in a hopeless situation. When the water is gone and the "infant" is crying, she places him under a bush and sits down a little distance away, because she can't bear to see him die. Hagar thinks her story—begun at the Well of the Living One Who Sees Me—is at an end. Her child, it appears, won't live to manhood, and she won't become the mother of a multitude after all.

And at that moment, the Living One Who Sees Her sees her again:

> *God heard the voice of the boy; and the angel of God called to Hagar from heaven, and said to her, "What troubles you, Hagar? Do not be afraid; for God has heard the voice of the boy where he is. Come, lift up the boy and hold him fast with your hand, for I will make a great nation of him." Then God opened her eyes and she saw a well of water. She went, and filled the skin with water, and gave the boy a drink. God was with the boy, and he grew up; he lived in the wilderness, and became an expert with the bow. He lived in the wilderness of Paran; and his mother got a wife for him from the land of Egypt. (Genesis 21:17–21)*

Not bad for a former slave-girl! It's Hagar who chooses the wife, securing the succession for her son by finding him a wife from among her own people. Again we see Hagar as a woman apart, one who acts outside the boundaries of normal conventions, who encounters God, who receives a direct revelation of God's promise, who names a well, and who does what's normally done only by men: she contracts a marriage for her son.

This is our final glimpse of Hagar—a woman who's moved light years from the powerless slave girl fleeing her mistress. She's achieved a genuine relationship with God, she's made a claim to property, and she's arranging a legal contract for her son. Not bad at all!

A Last Poignant Note

There's a final peculiar and poignant note in the story, that doesn't occur until much later. "Abraham breathed his last and died in a good old age, an old man and full of years, and was gathered to his people. His sons Isaac and Ishmael buried him in the cave of Machpelah" (Genesis 25:8–9).

What? After everything—the bitterness of Sarah and the helplessness of

Hagar, the near-death of Ishmael, left to die under a bush—we're brought up short, to say the least. Ishmael helping to bury Abraham? But Ishmael was sent away! Why would he suddenly reappear, on Abraham's death, when the future of Abraham's descendants now lies with Isaac?

Oh, but there's more. "After the death of Abraham God blessed his son Isaac. And Isaac settled at Beer-lahai-roi" (Genesis 25:11). Isaac is settling at the well claimed and named by Hagar, the well of Beer-lahai-roi, which will also figure later in Isaac's story.

Sarah, clearly, wasn't aware of everything that was going on when Abraham was out trading or wandering with the flocks. Even after the narration of Abraham's death, there's an equally long genealogy listing Ishmael's offspring right along with Isaac's.[6]

Sadly, we don't see Hagar again, but the greatness ascribed to her offspring leads us to believe that she picked the right wife for Ishmael, she managed the fortunes of her descendents, and—for someone who started off in the lowest possible position—she became a woman of substance and power.

FROM ISLAM: ANOTHER WAY OF SEEING HAGAR

Of the Five Pillars of Islam—the five duties required of adults Muslims—one is the Hajj, the pilgrimage to Mecca. Among the things that pilgrims must do are: ritually cast stones at a pillar of rock, drink from the well of Zamzam, and worship at the Ka'aba, the building that houses the Black Stone, a meteorite that God hurled to the earth. The story that follows is a retelling of a Sufi women's story, which explains the meaning of these actions, and memorializes the first one who performed them: not Ibrahim or Isma'il (Abraham or Ishmael), but Hagar, God's woman, the Mother of All Believers. Here, with thanks to the brothers and sisters who prayed and laughed with me in my Sufi days, is one version of that story.

This is the Story of Hagar. Remember it.

It all started with Sarah, really, and her hunger for a son. She would've done anything to get that son, even give her slave-girl Hagar to her husband. "You two give me a son," she said to them. Well, I don't think Abraham argued with her, and nobody would have listened to Hagar if she had.

And Hagar got pregnant, which is what Sarah wanted. But all of a sudden Sarah wasn't quite as pleased. For one thing, for the first time in her life, Hagar had something her mistress didn't have: a child in her womb. She was going to be the mother of the heir, and for all her trying Sarah had never achieved that. And Abraham was looking pretty pleased with himself about all this, too. After all, he was going to have a child, and at his age, too! He smiled at Hagar, and what man wouldn't?

It would've taken a stronger person than Hagar to resist the temptation to feel just a little bit pleased with herself, and to show it. Or maybe to feel a little bit sorry for her mistress, and to show that, too. Well, you know how Sarah liked that! She landed on Abraham with everything she had: "Now look what you've done! You've gotten my slave girl pregnant, and she's treating me like she was the Queen of Sheba. And it's all your fault!"

Well, of course, it was Abraham who got Hagar pregnant, but he wasn't the one who started things. But when Sarah was in one of her moods, you didn't want to cross her, so he just said, "You do whatever seems best to you." And what seemed best to Sarah was to treat Hagar worse than she'd ever been treated in her life.

Hagar took about as much as she could, and then she just ran away. She went out into the wilderness and sat down at a well. Maybe she was hoping somebody would come along and take her away. And somebody did come along, but it wasn't anybody she'd ever seen before.

God's angel came up to her and said, "Hagar! What on earth are you doing out here in the wilderness? You're going to starve to death out here!"

"I don't care," said Hagar. "It's better than what I've been through these last few weeks." And she just sat there.

"Look," said the angel, "this isn't the thing to do. That baby you're carrying is very important. If you die he won't get born, and it's important that he gets born. His offspring will be great princes and warriors. They'll be special to God. You go on home to Sarah, and stay alive so this child can get born."

Hagar just shook her head. "You don't know what that woman's like," she said.

"Well, yes I do," said the angel. "I can't promise you she's going to go all lovey-dovey on you. She's probably going to go on the same way. So I'm not telling you to go back. I'm asking you. Please go back. What can I offer you to get you to go back?"

Hagar looked the angel right in the eye. "What can you offer me? My freedom, that's what you can offer me."

The angel scratched his head. "Well, that's a really hard one to do, Hagar. That's a very expensive thing. It isn't easy. But here, here's a token of God's promise to do the best to get you your freedom." And the angel reached down and took three stones from the desert floor at his feet, and he handed them to Hagar.

"These are the three gifts of the heart," he said. "The first is Love, and the second is Courage, and the third is Will. Nobody on earth ever really has freedom that hasn't got these three gifts. So you take these, and go home and have your baby."

So Hagar went home, carrying the three stones, and before you knew it, she'd given birth to her son Ishmael. Abraham loved that boy, too, nearly as much as Hagar did. But Sarah, she wasn't at all happy, even though it was her doing in the first place.

Well, finally, after a long time, Sarah got pregnant, too, and had her son Isaac. And as soon as she knew she had a son of her own, she could hardly wait to get rid of Hagar and her son.

"You get that woman and her son out of here," she said to Abraham. "I don't want him inheriting what should belong to my boy." Well, Abraham wasn't all that happy about this, because Ishmael was his son, too, and the thought of having to throw the two of them out to die was just too much. But God came to Abraham in a dream and said, "Don't worry, Abraham. I take care of my own. I'll take care of Hagar and Ishmael. I won't forget them." And so Abraham knew he had to do what Sarah said.

So early the next morning, he took a water skin, and a bag of food, and set them on Hagar's shoulder and sent her and Ishmael away into the wilderness.

Hagar walked a long way that first morning, and when she sat down to rest, Satan came along and sat down beside her. "Doesn't it just fry you, Hagar, the way they've treated you? Wouldn't you really love to get your own back?"

"Well, yes, who wouldn't?" Hagar said.

"If you just throw in with me, I'll see to it that you get your revenge. You serve me and I'll take care of that woman for you."

Hagar snorted. "Oh, you're all heart, aren't you? One master just tossed me out, and I'm supposed to turn around and be your slave instead? No way! I *will* go on my way." And with that, she took the first stone, the stone of Will, and she threw it straight at the Devil. It whacked him right in the eye.

Satan just kept smiling. "OK, I get the point. You'll get good sense sooner or later. You haven't seen the last of me." And he disappeared.

Hagar kept walking, that day, and the next day, and the next one after that. And the water skin was starting to look pretty empty, and the food bag was looking emptier still, and she didn't see any wells or oases. And on the next day, Satan came back again, and walked alongside her.

"Not very much water left, is there, Hagar? Not much food, either. If I were you, I'd be feeling a little scared. If you were to serve me, now, I'd see you had plenty to eat and drink."

Hagar said, "I'm scared, all right, but I don't need you. God gave me courage." And she took the second stone, the stone called Courage, and threw it right in his face.

Satan narrowed his eyes. "I'm a patient sort, Hagar. I'm not giving up. You'll see me again." And he disappeared.

Well, the water was gone, and the food was gone. And pretty soon her strength was gone too. There was nothing as far as she could see, except a few vultures up there, circling around and just waiting. And Satan came back.

"Where's your God now, Hagar?" he asked. "Don't you know he's deserted you? He's not going to save you. You're going to die out here in the wilderness. I'm the only one who can help you now. Without me, you'll die."

And Hagar said, "Yes, I'm going to die. But you know, that's not the worst thing that can happen. I'm not ever going to go with you, not ever. Do you know why? Because once, a long time ago, God asked me to do something. God *asked* me. All my life, I was a slave and people *told* me to do this and do that. God was the only one who ever *asked* me. In all my life, nobody ever loved me that much before. And because of that love, I'll always be God's woman. *Great is God; there is no God but God!*"

And she took the third stone, the stone called Love, and threw it into the face of Satan. And when it struck him, he was frozen into a pillar of rock. And God looked down and saw Hagar there, and he heard her cry, and God caught a flaming stone out of the heavens and hurled it down to earth, and it landed at her feet. And where the rock struck, water sprang up, a great well gushing up at her feet.

And Hagar fell on her face in terror, because she knew she was in the presence of the Holy One. But God took her by the hand, and said, "Stand up, Hagar. Don't be afraid. You are no one's slave any more. You are my woman, a free woman. I will make this wilderness a refuge for you and your children, and people will tell this story about you as long as there are people in this world."

And Hagar stood up, a free woman, God's woman, the Mother of All Believers, and the first of those who turned her face to Mecca.

This is the Story of Hagar. Remember it.[7]

Yes, the way Sufi women have told the story is a bit different than the way Genesis tells it, though it centers on the same character: a woman, who is expected to bear a child for another woman, is harshly mistreated and eventually cast out to die with her son in the wilderness. But stories, you know, are not simply histories of *events*, but the histories of *meanings* as well. In the Genesis version, the meaning of Hagar's journey is embedded in Abraham's saga: God is keeping faith with an earlier promise to establish a great nation from the descendents of Abraham, through the long-awaited son Isaac. God will rescue the boy Ishmael and his mother *for Abraham's sake*, but it is the boy God hears, not Hagar.

> *And God heard the voice of the boy; and the angel of God called to Hagar from heaven, and said to her, "What troubles you, Hagar? Do not be afraid; for God has heard the voice of the boy where he is. Come, lift up the boy and hold him fast with your hand, for I will make a great nation of him." Then God opened her eyes and she saw a well of water. She went, and filled the skin with water, and gave the boy a drink. (Genesis 21:17–19)*

In the Sufi version, on the other hand, the meaning is quite different: Hagar's story is not simply embedded in Abraham's or in Ishmael's. The story is her own, and in some ways emblematic of every believer's journey. She is the woman who seeks freedom, and who risks her life to achieve it. She crosses the wilderness, contends with Satan, resists his temptations, and remains faithful to her earlier encounter with God. The gifts of will, courage, and love have deep meaning for many Sufi orders: they are the indispensable gifts of the heart without which no one can reach the end of the long pilgrimage to God.

The Sufi tale is not the Genesis version of the story, true, but in its very essence it is a story that speaks with a universal voice, the story of what many women have learned in their hard roads to freedom: it is a costly journey that takes will, courage, and above all, love.

But it is a journey that is made with the best and most faithful of companions: God.

ROBERTA'S STORY

My great-great-grandmother's name was Ivy. Just Ivy. She was born a slave, somewhere in Alabama, probably around 1847 or 1848, and she didn't have a last name, unless it was her owner's name, but I don't recall ever hearing that. She would never talk much about that part of her life. I always imagined it was just nothing she cared to remember, and who can wonder why?

When the Civil War ended, and Emancipation came, Ivy was sixteen or seventeen. She was what we'd call a teenager nowadays, but that's a word that really wouldn't have fit her. At sixteen, she was a grown-up woman who had already known her share of burdens. She had already given birth to one child, and was carrying a second one. She didn't have a husband, and she would never talk about who the father of her children was, whether it was the man who owned her or another slave or whoever. To my knowledge, she never even told her children, just said things like, "That's all past, now, we got to live today if we want to see tomorrow." My grandmother said that Ivy used to say, in a very fierce voice, "God gave me those babies and I knew the Lord'd give me the strength to keep 'em. And I meant to keep 'em!" That was Ivy! God gave her those babies, and she'd do whatever she had to do to take care of them.

When I hear Hagar's story, I can't help but think of Ivy. Whoever got Hagar pregnant, that wasn't even important to her. It was God who gave her that son and she meant to keep him alive. I don't think she really spent any time repining over Abraham, and I don't even know that she was sorry about being sent away. At least she didn't have to stay around to be Sarah's slave, or to see her boy live in Isaac's shadow forever.

Ivy, when the war ended and she found out she was a free woman, thought first of all of her son and the baby she was carrying. She wanted them to grow up free, in a place where their mother had never been a slave. So this woman, with no family, who never learned to read or write, who didn't even know her own birth date or birth place for certain, set out to build a life for herself and her children. She started walking north, carrying her toddler on her hip and all her belongings on her back.

She was a country woman, a strong woman who'd done hard work in the fields, and knew how to milk a cow and churn butter and all that sort of thing, so she was able to get work along the way. Finally, when she got as far north as Ohio, she met a Mennonite family who were moving west to homestead, and they took her along as hired help. When my great-grandfather was born, she gave him the name Lincoln after the President, and took the family name "Walker," because she said that's what she was, a woman walking to keep her babies from knowing the misery she had known in her life.

That was the whole thing that mattered to Ivy. God had given her those babies and she was going to hold God to the promise to give her the strength to keep them. Between them, I think God and Ivy were a pretty powerful combination. That woman worked as hard as any man in the fields, and she didn't stop there. She took on extra work, too, so that her boys wouldn't have to go to the fields and could go to school with the Mennonite children instead. That was one ambitious woman! Not for herself, mind you, but for her children. She moved her family three times over the years, each time to give her children—and then later her grandchildren—more opportunities. She never did learn to read or write, but she saw two of her grandchildren graduate from teacher's college, and just a few weeks before she died, her great-grandson hung up his shingle as the first African American doctor in his community.

I know her life—especially her early life as a slave—was full of pain and grief and unbelievable hard work, and yes, I think we need to remember the injustice of what was done to Ivy and women like her. But that's only half the story. The other half is what she handed on to us by her example. She had that fierce belief that God had given her those children and the strength to keep them, with or without a family, a husband, or a world that was free and fair-minded. Nothing in the world was stronger than Ivy Walker, her faith, and her God.

I have a life that's so much better than hers, there's really no comparison. Here I am, an educated woman with a caring husband and a good job, living in a comfortable home of my own with every *laborsaving thing you can think of. No cows to milk, no laundry to boil, no trudging in the snow in broken down shoes. But let me tell you, I am just pure Ivy Walker when it comes to my grandson! God gave me that boy to raise and I'm no different than Ivy—I mean to keep him. And God help anybody who tries to get in the way of my doing that. I've got God and Ivy Walker on my side.*

QUESTIONS FOR STUDY AND REFLECTION

In reading the story:
- What is Hagar's position? Problems and desires? Personality?
- What makes her tick?
- What strengths does she have? What flaws?
- What is her relationship with God at the start of the story?
- How does this relationship appear to develop?
- Where is she at the end of the story?

Self-reflection and learning:
- What in my life has resembled Hagar's?
- How have I dealt with problems in ways similar to hers?
- What light does she throw on my own story?
- Has someone else played Hagar in my life?
- How have Hagar's "three gifts" worked in my life?

What questions and problems does this still leave unanswered or "in process"?

CHAPTER FOUR

The Invisible Man and the Managing Woman, or "Mother Knows Best"

By now, we've heard more about Abraham and his family than we bargained for, but we're not done yet. Before we move on to the next story—that of Rebekah, one of the most memorable of all memorable women in the Old Testament—let's take a close look at some background scenes that explain much of what we'll see in the story to come.

Let's begin by going back to Genesis 22, the so-called sacrifice of Isaac. This is one of the most difficult passages in the Old Testament because of the grim questions it raises about the nature of God and the nature of humanity's relationship to God. Modern people tend to ask, "Was God really serious about this?" and "Why would God test Abraham so cruelly? He's been tormenting him for years about this promised child, and now . . . !" The story also raises tough questions about what it takes to be a follower of God, considering that Abraham's unquestioning obedience has traditionally been held up as an example of admirable faith.

God begins by reminding Abraham how much he loves Isaac.

> *After these things God tested Abraham. He said to him, "Abraham!"*
> *And he said, "Here I am." He said, "Take your son, your only son*
> *Isaac, whom you love . . . and go to the land of Moriah, and offer*
> *him there as a burnt offering on one of the mountains that*
> *I shall show you." (Genesis 22:1–2)*

After all the years of waiting for this child, and all Abraham's doubts about whether there would ever be a child, and all the time Abraham spent nagging God about it, and the agonies of Abraham reminding God that he doesn't have a son, and God saying, "No, no, it's OK. You'll have descendents more numerous than the stars in the sky." It takes until Abraham is a hundred and his wife is ninety before this miraculous child is born. And now God asks the unthinkable.

> *So Abraham rose early in the morning, saddled his donkey, and took two of his young men with him, and his son Isaac; he cut the wood for the burnt offering, and set out and went to the place in the distance that God had shown him. (Genesis 22:3)*

Genesis doesn't tell us whether Abraham told Sarah what was going on, but can anyone picture Sarah just sitting by and letting Abraham do this, God or no? Considering how forthright she's been up to now, I have a feeling that if she'd thought Abraham was threatening her boy, *he* would have been a burnt offering, or at least toast.

The story shows us, instead, a furtive and heart-wrenching expedition.

> *On the third day Abraham looked up and saw the place far away. Then Abraham said to his young men, "Stay here with the donkey; the boy and I will go over there; we will worship, and then we will come back to you." Abraham took the wood of the burnt offering and laid it on his son Isaac, and he himself carried the fire and the knife. So the two of them walked on together. Isaac said to his father Abraham, "Father!" And he said, "Here I am, my son." He said, "The fire and the wood are here, but where is the lamb for a burnt offering?" Abraham said, "God himself will provide the lamb for a burnt offering, my son." So the two of them walked on together.*
> *(Genesis 22:4–8)*

Abraham, by this time, is barely speaking, even to his son—and small wonder. The scene is horrifyingly heavy with irony and unspoken pain. He cannot be honest either with the servants who have come with them, or with the boy himself.

We don't know for certain how old Isaac is at this point, but since he's old enough to be capable of carrying a bundle of wood sufficient to burn a human being on, he is not a small child who won't understand what's going on. He's old enough to recognize what is going on. And therein lies some of the awfulness of the scene.

> *When they came to the place that God had shown him, Abraham built an altar there and laid the wood in order. He bound his son Isaac, and laid him on the altar, on top of the wood. Then Abraham reached out his hand and took the knife to kill his son.*
> *(Genesis 22:9–10)*

This is masterful narration; you can practically feels the listeners holding their breath.

> *But the angel of the LORD called to him from heaven, and said, "Abraham, Abraham!" And he said, "Here I am." He said, "Do not lay your hand on the boy or do anything to him; for now I know that you fear God, since you have not withheld your son, your only son, from me." And Abraham looked up and saw a ram, caught in a thicket by its horns. Abraham went and took the ram and offered it up as a burnt offering instead of his son. So Abraham called that place "The LORD will provide"; as it is said to this day, "On the mount of the LORD it shall be provided." (Genesis 22:11–14)*

THE REAL PROBLEM

This is a real problem passage, and there are all kinds of theories about it. Is God indicating that the sacrifice of children will no longer be permitted, in a time and a culture where the sacrifice of children was still deplorably common? But what kind of God would put Abraham through the agony of all this? If God is testing Abraham's faith, hasn't he tested the poor soul long enough by now? Given the intimacy of their relationship, it seems impossible that God couldn't already know the quality of Abraham's character.

I see this passage as the remnant of a much older, more primitive story that's been interwoven in the Abraham saga, too time-honored to be discarded by the Old Testament storytellers, however ill it fit with a more sophisticated image of a caring and compassionate God. Such remnants do exist—the passage in which God inexplicably tries to kill Moses in the middle of the night, for instance.

> *On the way, at a place where they spent the night, the LORD met him and tried to kill him. But Zipporah took a flint and cut off her son's foreskin, and touched Moses' feet [genitals] with it, and said, "Truly you are a bridegroom of blood to me!" So [God] let him alone.*
> *(Exodus 4:24–26)*

This is simply a fragment of a very primitive picture of God, much older than the rest of the surrounding narrative. Probably most hearers no longer even knew what it signified by the time the Old Testament was compiled.

These are primitive remnants, but their impact as story is still astonishing. We're brought into the presence of a frightening, mysterious, all-powerful God, whose will can't be fathomed and whose intentions can't even be grasped. And yet they shape the story in powerful ways. From our standpoint, we see Isaac, a child of promise, old enough to understand what's going on and to feel the same fear the reader feels. He must know he's come within inches of being slaughtered and burnt as an offering to his father's God. Frankly, if I were Isaac, I think I'd have become an atheist.

In fact, when we pause to look at the subsequent story, it's obvious that Isaac doesn't have the kind of relationship with God that his father does. Abraham and God talk as if they were friends, while Isaac lies low, as if hoping God won't notice him. Isaac, in short, is the Invisible Man, lacking the strong personality of his father or his sons. It's almost as if he's been so terrified by God that he never wanted anything to do with anything spiritual again. Neither would I, come to think of it.

I think we have to take that into account here. Isaac, in this whole string of stories, isn't really an *actor*. First he's the child everybody waits for, whose birth signifies something momentous. He disappears into Sarah's tent and emerges only on state occasions, like his weaning. Then he becomes a kind of token tossed between his father and God—the means of God proving whether or not Abraham believes enough. He's the symbol of the favor that God gives Abraham. He's the symbol of the blessing God gives at last to Sarah.

Does God have anything to say to Isaac? Does Isaac have a life of his own? The God of the mountaintop on Moriah isn't a God who invites intimacy. He may provide a last-minute ram in the thicket, but only after making the young would-be victim endure an unforgivable agony of fear.

For me, one of the most horrifying poems that's come out of our own troubled centuries—because it shows so clearly where the primitive root of this vision of God remains in our own religion and culture—is Wilfred Owen's World War I retelling of the Abraham and Isaac story, a glimpse of how easily this strand of belief became warped to the service of madness.

The Parable of the Old Man and the Young

> So Abram rose, and clave the wood, and went,
> And took the fire with him, and a knife.
> And as they sojourned both of them together,
> Isaac the first-born spake and said, My Father,
> Behold the preparations, fire and iron,
> But where the lamb, for this burnt-offering?
> Then Abram bound the youth with belts and straps,
> And builded parapets and trenches there,
> And stretchèd forth the knife to slay his son.
> When lo! An Angel called him out of heaven,
> Saying, Lay not thy hand upon the lad,
> Neither do anything to him, thy son.
> Behold! Caught in a thicket by its horns,
> A Ram. Offer the Ram of Pride instead.

But the old man would not so, but slew his son,
And half the seed of Europe, one by one.
(1918)[8]

"THE FEAR OF ISAAC"

You may begin to see that something odd has happened in the thread of the story. Here's a God who was so close to Adam and Eve, even after the fall. A God who spoke as a friend to Abraham, who was not afraid to bargain with God over the fate of Sodom. But something changes in the quality of human-God relationships in this chilling passage—or perhaps in the *perception* of human-God relationships. In part, of course, this is simply where a different story tradition took up, but for the sake of the subsequent story, we should point out that for a son so fervently awaited and so important to God, Isaac is really something of a puzzle. He's the Invisible Man, keeping such a low profile that we barely get a glimpse of his personality. We have a very clear picture of what Abraham is like, and what Sarah is like, even what Hagar is like. But Isaac hardly ever speaks and doesn't make waves—possibly because of what might happen if you attract God's attention. If the future of Israel were left to Isaac, at this point, it would be grim news indeed: the thread of communication between God and humanity comes close to being snapped.

Isaac apparently goes back to Sarah's tent and gives both his father and God a wide berth. In fact, much later in Genesis, in the midst of Jacob's story, two interesting and possibly revelatory passages occur. In his confrontation with his father-in-law Laban, Jacob says, "If the God of my father, the God of Abraham and the Fear of Isaac, had not been on my side, surely now you would have sent me away empty-handed" (Genesis 31:42). Further on, "[Laban said], 'May the God of Abraham and the God of Nahor'—the God of their father—'judge between us.' So Jacob swore by the Fear of his father Isaac" (Genesis 31:53). The God of Abraham, but the *Fear* of Isaac. Small wonder that we see and hear nothing of Isaac again until he is thirty-seven years old, and his mother has just died.

Now Abraham was old, well advanced in years; and the LORD *had*
blessed Abraham in all things. Abraham said to his servant, the oldest
of his house, who had charge of all that he had, "Put your hand
under my thigh and I will make you swear by the LORD, *the God of*
heaven and earth, that you will not get a wife for my son from the
daughters of the Canaanites, among whom I live, but will go to my
country and to my kindred and get a wife for my son Isaac."
(Genesis 24:1–4)

Asking the servant to put his hand under Abraham's thigh is a way of swearing very solemnly by putting his hand on Abraham's genitals. It's way more solemn than pinky swearing or spitting in your hand, which was about as adventurous as we got as kids. But then, they were rather careful as to what parts of the Bible we were allowed to read.

Note here that all of the business of Isaac's marriage will be taken care of by others: Isaac remains the Invisible Man throughout the courtship and marriage contracting—thirty-seven years old or no.

> Abraham said to him, "See to it that you do not take my son back there. The LORD, the God of heaven, who took me from my father's house and from the land of my birth, and who spoke to me and swore to me, 'To your offspring I will give this land,' he will send his angel before you, and you shall take a wife for my son from there."
> (Genesis 24:6–8)

While it's perfectly true that the heads of families arranged for marriages for their offspring, the idea of a man still being unmarried at thirty-seven is almost unheard of, especially in that progeny-obsessed culture. Was Isaac Sarah's boy for this long? We can't really tell, but the implication is that Isaac remained unusually close to his mother, and only at her death did Abraham think of getting him a wife.

In any event, Abraham does the thing handsomely: he sends the servant off with ten camels, all loaded with gifts, a veritable caravan (Genesis 24:10). Now, there's a major anachronism here. At the actual time of the story, camels were not common in that part of the Middle East; donkeys were the primary animals used for trading and traveling. When camels were introduced they were quite exotic and very, very expensive. Having ten camels would have been roughly the equivalent of having twenty Rolls Royces, when most folks of the day couldn't even afford a used Chevy. Clearly, the narrator wants us to understand that Abraham is very, very wealthy. The servant takes wealth upon wealth—making sure we understand that these are only *part* of Abraham's herd of camels—and goes to Aram-naharaim, the city where Abraham's brother Nahor lives.

An Anything-But-Modest Young Woman

The meeting of Rebekah and her future father-in-law's servant is full of hints that may be lost on us, but must have made the story's original hearers raise their eyebrows. "He made the camels kneel down outside the city by the well of water; it was toward evening, the time when women go out to draw water" (Genesis 24:11). Hint 1: The time people draw water from wells is very significant. Ordinary housewives drew it in the morning, because they needed water for the tasks of the day. The Samaritan woman in the gospel of John went to the well at noon, and met Jesus there. Being there alone at noon was a hint that she was probably something of a social outcaste, avoided by the other women. In other words, she didn't go when the decent, self-respecting women of her neighborhood did. Abraham's servant seems blissfully unaware of what to expect; being a male servant he no doubt never draws water at the well anyway.

> And he said, "O LORD, God of my master Abraham, please grant me success today and show steadfast love to my master Abraham. I am standing here by the spring of water, and the daughters of the townspeople are coming out to draw water. Let the girl to whom I shall say, 'Please offer your jar that I may drink,' and who shall say, 'Drink, and I will water your camels'—let her be the one whom you have appointed for your servant Isaac. By this I shall know that you have shown steadfast love to my master." (Genesis 24:12–14)

Both the servant and the reader need reassurance that the right woman will be chosen.

He hardly has the words out of his mouth when Rebekah arrives, right on cue. We learn immediately that she's the daughter of Abraham's nephew Bethuel, that she's a knockout and that she's a virgin.

> She went down to the spring, filled her jar, and came up. Then the servant ran to meet her and said, "Please let me sip a little water from your jar." "Drink, my lord," she said, and quickly lowered her jar upon her hand and gave him a drink. When she had finished giving him a drink, she said, "I will draw for your camels also, until they have finished drinking." So she quickly emptied her jar into the trough and ran again to the well to draw, and she drew for all his camels. (Genesis 24:16–20)

Do you know how much water it takes to fill ten camels? The listeners probably knew, and were probably shaking their heads by this time at the thought of the girl running back and forth thirty or forty times with her water jar.

But that's not what would really have surprised them. Look at this picture through their eyes. Here's this absolute stranger, clearly very wealthy, with ten camels in tow. He's not driving a beat-up '81 Datsun, he's not a hitchhiker: he's got *ten camels*. Moreover, this is a culture in which well-brought-up young women don't speak to strangers, much less offer to water their camels. It doesn't sound to me like Rebekah's in any real big hurry to get home.

Next, there's no hint that anyone else is around: this girl is absolutely—and unthinkably—on her own. And if there are other women around—older women who are watching this exchange—you can imagine what they're thinking or saying. All you have to do is picture the average small town. This is shameless behavior!

Now, even at this point we're beginning to get a picture of Rebekah that tells us she isn't exactly a violet by a mossy stone. She's not some shy little thing who's afraid to speak to strangers. She takes the bit right in her teeth—after all, this is a small town, and it's probably pretty boring, and here is somebody new and interesting.

> *When the camels had finished drinking, the man took a gold nose-ring weighing a half shekel, and two bracelets for her arms weighing ten gold shekels. (Genesis 24:22)*

Now all told, he is loading about two pounds of gold on her here. People don't even earn that kind of money in a year.

> *And [he] said, "Tell me whose daughter you are. Is there room in your father's house for us to spend the night?" She said to him, "I am the daughter of Bethuel son of Milcah, whom she bore to Nahor." She added, "We have plenty of straw and fodder and a place to spend the night." (Genesis 24:23–25)*

We see something else about Rebekah here: *she* invites this stranger to her house. She doesn't consult Mom and Dad. She's watered the camels, and she's volunteering the hospitality of her parents' home in a culture in which that is taken very, very seriously. The guest is sacred. It's far more significant than it is in our culture. This isn't just asking someone to drop in for a cup of coffee. It's extending the honor of the family to the newcomer.

Rebekah may not be the properly modest young thing, but she fit the exact specs the servant spelled out to God. Obviously this is the one. (Why God would choose someone like this will become apparent later on in the story.) Moreover, the servant now knows that this is a proper match for Isaac, because she's related to Abraham's brother Nahor.

"Then the girl ran and told her mother's household about these things" (Genesis 24:28). Notice that. Her mother's household, not her father's household. Where's Dad? Is this a family in which the father has several wives and has established separate households for them? Or is Mom the property owner here? We'll see who's in charge in a few verses, and it certainly isn't Dad.

Now we're treated to one of the most delicious portraits in the Old Testament, that of Laban, Rebekah's brother. Let the story speak for itself.

> *Rebekah had a brother whose name was Laban; and Laban ran out to the man, to the spring. As soon as he had seen the nose-ring, and*

the bracelets on his sister's arms, and when he heard the words of his
sister Rebekah, "Thus the man spoke to me," he went to the man; and
there he was, standing by the camels at the spring. He said, "Come in,
O blessed of the LORD. Why do you stand outside when I have
prepared the house and a place for the camels?" (Genesis 24:29–31)

This is the original wheeler-dealer. It may even be a whole houseful of
wheeler-dealers. Laban takes one look at the loot his sister is loaded down
with, and he's out the door like a shot.

This bunch knows what side their camels are buttered on, and Rebekah
knows a wealthy man when she sees one. Laban has probably already assessed
the market value of the bracelets on his sister's arms. This first glimpse of
Laban will come to mind later, when he appears in the Jacob story. Laban is
your basic sharpie.

If we translate this into twenty-first-century terms, Rebekah isn't the shy
type who's hanging around the house all day stirring the beans. She's out
seeing what's going on—what's new. Maybe she's impressed by the camels,
but the very novelty of somebody new in town appeals to her. Again, look at
Laban: "He said, 'Come in, O blessed of the LORD. Why do you stand outside
when I have prepared the house and a place for the camels?' I, Laban. Not
Mom, not Dad. But me, I, who never even knew you existed till ten seconds
ago. Does it begin to sound as if the kids are running this house? So far Mom
and Dad haven't even appeared, except by inference.

So the man came into the house; and Laban unloaded the camels,
and gave him straw and fodder for the camels, and water to wash his
feet and the feet of the men who were with him. (Genesis 24:32)

Now, at last, the servant tells in minute detail the story of his master, how
wealthy he is, and how admirable, and how God has answered Abraham's
prayer and his own. Partly, he's trying to reinforce the idea that this is God's
doing, of course, so that the family will agree to the match. Only at this point,
finally, does Dad (Bethuel) speak up: "... take her and go..." (Genesis 24:51).
Up till now, Rebekah and Laban have clearly been running the household. It's
possible that Bethuel is simply tired of trying to cope with his offspring, or at
least he doesn't seem to think he has much choice in the matter. This is
another of those oddly un-patriarchal pictures we're given. The household is
that of Rebekah's mother, the girl and her brother do all the haggling, and all
Bethuel seems to be needed for is to sign the contract. Not patriarchy the way
we've been taught to expect it.

When Abraham's servant heard these words, he bowed himself to the
ground before the LORD. And the servant brought out jewelry of silver

and of gold, and garments, and gave them to Rebekah; he also gave to
her brother and to her mother costly ornaments. (Genesis 24:52–53)

Why are we not surprised that he ignores Dad, too? No camels or jewelry
for Dad; he knows who to flatter.

Next morning, the servant presses Laban and his mother to give him
Rebekah and send them on their way. Note that now it's Laban and Mama,
not Bethuel. So they call Rebekah and ask her if she's ready to go with this
man, and Rebekah—in a world in which travel is fairly rare, and it's likely
she'll never see her family again—doesn't hesitate for one-tenth of a second
(Genesis 24:54–61).

So Rebekah sets off, with her nurse and "her maids," apparently a woman
of property and status. She has attendants and at least one personal servant.
She's not a little nobody.

There's something else interesting in this passage. Have you noticed it?
The servant refers to his master, Abraham, and how wealthy he is, but never
mentions the Invisible Man, Isaac. Not really. Rebekah and her family hear all
about Abraham, and nothing about Isaac. He might have two heads for all
they know—or apparently care. Rebekah has heard nothing about the man
she's going to marry, and yet she's ready to go as soon as the opportunity
presents itself. This may say as much about home as it does about Rebekah.

Now Isaac had come from Beer-lahai-roi [remember, this was
Hagar's well], and was settled in the Negeb. Isaac went out in the
evening to walk in the field; and looking up, he saw camels coming.
And Rebekah looked up, and when she saw Isaac, she slipped quickly
from the camel, and said to the servant, "Who is the man over there,
walking in the field to meet us?" The servant said, "It is my master."
So she took her veil and covered herself. (Genesis 24:62–65)

Veiling herself doesn't mean that Rebekah is a shy little bride. I have a
feeling she's going to play the woman of mystery to intrigue Isaac.

And the servant told Isaac all the things that he had done. Then Isaac
brought her into his mother Sarah's tent. He took Rebekah, and she
became his wife; and he loved her. So Isaac was comforted after his
mother's death. (Genesis 24:66–67)

Notice, he takes Rebekah to the tent of his mother, the headwoman—an
important place to him, since Sarah is dead and yet her tent is preserved.

I'm afraid it does sound a little like a young man looking for another
Mama, somebody to replace his mother, doesn't it? And what we've seen so
far in Rebekah, I don't think she's going to have any problems taking on the

adult role in this family—she tossed aside the child's role a long time ago. But Isaac is still the Invisible Man.

The Plot Thickens

Presently Abraham dies, and at the age of forty, Isaac becomes the head of the family. But—same song, second verse—God's promise is again threatened by the inability of Rebekah to have a child. Isaac has to pray to God for Rebekah (a thing he probably enjoys doing the way most of us enjoy having a root canal) so that she'll be able to have a child. Rebekah not only conceives, but she conceives twins, and even before they're born, we get the feeling that these kids won't be a Norman Rockwell pair.

> *The children struggled together within her; and she said, "If it is to be this way, why do I live?" So she went to inquire of the LORD.*
> *And the LORD said to her,*
> *"Two nations are in your womb,*
> *and two peoples born of you shall be divided;*
> *the one shall be stronger than the other,*
> *the elder shall serve the younger."*
> *When her time to give birth was at hand, there were twins in her womb. The first came out red, all his body like a hairy mantle; so they named him Esau. Afterward his brother came out, with his hand gripping Esau's heel; so he was named Jacob. Isaac was sixty years old when she bore them. When the boys grew up, Esau was a skillful hunter, a man of the field, while Jacob was a quiet man, living in tents. Isaac loved Esau, because he was fond of game; but Rebekah loved Jacob." (Genesis 25:22–28)*

Here's the classic story we all heard in Sunday School, not to mention the classic story of many a novel. Notice first that Isaac loved Esau "because he was fond of game." Huh? It makes you wonder if Isaac had a few problems relating to people altogether, including his own sons. "What do I love about my son? He brings me game." Here's Daddy's boy, clearly. If he lived in this century, he'd be out playing football, hunting deer, and driving an S.U.V. Maybe it appealed to Isaac, who never seems to have gotten away from his mother long enough to do any of those guy things.

But of course, Rebekah loves Jacob. Naturally. If nothing else, the story demands it. (For one thing, it's difficult picturing a live wire like Rebekah doting on a son whose greatest virtue is that he can kill small animals.)

Now notice the next episode in story, "*Once when Jacob was cooking a stew—*" Say what? Note that, please. This is a patriarchal culture, and Jacob is in the tent whipping up a little stew?

> *Once when Jacob was cooking a stew, Esau came in from the field,
> and he was famished. Esau said to Jacob, "Let me eat some of that
> red stuff, for I am famished!" (Therefore he was called Edom.) Jacob
> said, "First sell me your birthright." Esau said, "I am about to die; of
> what use is a birthright to me?" Jacob said, "Swear to me first." So he
> swore to him, and sold his birthright to Jacob. Then Jacob gave Esau
> bread and lentil stew, and he ate and drank, and rose and went his
> way. Thus Esau despised his birthright. (Genesis 25:29–34)*

The narrator has given us the portraits of these two brothers with incredible economy. First, it's unlikely that Esau was actually dying of hunger; more likely he was just really hungry after a hard morning running around in the fields and wanted his lunch *now*. There were probably servants who could've whipped something up for him without demanding his birthright. But no, he wants it *now*—he seems to have a little trouble deferring gratification. And he's not the sharpest one in the family, while Jacob, at least as we see him in this scene, is clearly the nephew of Laban, capable of a little wheeling-dealing. Maybe it's just his nature, or maybe it's something he's learned along the way from his mother, the daughter of a very sharp family.

Re-Playing an Older Script

Let's just slide by Genesis 26 here, another example of the editors falling asleep at the switch. It's the same story as the two earlier incidents in which Abraham passes Sarah off as his sister, only this time it's Isaac and Rebekah, and even the location remains unchanged—we're back with King Abimelech in Gerar. But there's an interesting difference. Isaac tells the men of that country that Rebekah is his sister, but he doesn't consult Rebekah about it, as Abraham did with Sarah. This time God doesn't actually interfere, but in a scene right out of a French farce, King Abimelech looks out of the window and sees Isaac fondling his wife. Abimelech, who must be getting heartily tired of this family by now, doesn't give Isaac flocks and herds, as he had to Abraham. But he does give the family their walking papers. End of episode. Isaac couldn't even carry it off as slickly as his father.

Toward the end of that chapter, we get another little glimpse of Esau—again, not a very admirable one. "When Esau was forty years old, he married Judith daughter of Beeri the Hittite, and Basemath daughter of Elon the Hittite; and they made life bitter for Isaac and Rebekah" (Genesis 26:34–35). Notice anything here? Esau really is kind of a dim bulb. He not only goes off and marries on his own, in a culture where your family is supposed to arrange marriages for you, but he goes outside the kinship group to do it. He marries a pair of Hittite women. True, they're not exactly the biblical version of trailer trash, but recall how particular Abraham had been about making sure his own son married a woman of his own family line.

What, we may ask, is going to happen to the promise that God made to Abraham about his descendents? Is the land going to go to half-Hittite offspring? This is not good news, clearly. Esau is threatening to subvert God's plan. Then, too, his Hittite wives made life bitter for Isaac and Rebekah. Being a sort of managerial woman, I don't doubt that Rebekah was *not* pleased with having a couple of daughters-in-law she hadn't chosen herself. Esau, clearly, didn't get it.

The Well-Known Scene Revisited

Now, here we come to another well-known scene we all *think* we know, but listen very carefully to the next part of the story. You may see something you weren't expecting.

> *When Isaac was old and his eyes were dim so that he could not see,*
> *he called his elder son Esau and said to him, "My son"; and he*
> *answered, "Here I am." He said, "See, I am old; I do not know the*
> *day of my death. Now then, take your weapons, your quiver and your*
> *bow, and go out to the field, and hunt game for me. Then prepare for*
> *me savory food, such as I like, and bring it to me to eat, so that I may*
> *bless you before I die." (Genesis 27:1–4)*

Now remember, the only thing we know Isaac likes about his son is the fact that he hunts game for him, so this is a fairly important commission. Or maybe it's just the only commission Isaac knows Esau can get right.

> *Now Rebekah was listening when Isaac spoke to his son Esau. So*
> *when Esau went to the field to hunt for game and bring it, Rebekah*
> *said to her son Jacob, "I heard your father say to your brother Esau,*
> *'Bring me game, and prepare for me savory food to eat, that I may*
> *bless you before the LORD before I die.' Now therefore, my son, obey*
> *my word as I command you. Go to the flock, and get me two choice*
> *kids, so that I may prepare from them savory food for your father,*
> *such as he likes; and you shall take it to your father to eat, so that he*
> *may bless you before he dies." But Jacob said to his mother Rebekah,*
> *"Look, my brother Esau is a hairy man, and I am a man of smooth*
> *skin. Perhaps my father will feel me, and I shall seem to be mocking*
> *him, and bring a curse on myself and not a blessing." His mother said*
> *to him, "Let your curse be on me, my son; only obey my word, and*
> *go, get them for me." (Genesis 27:5–13)*

Most of us came out of Sunday School thinking that Jacob was the cheater here, scheming to get his brother's blessing. But when we look at the story it's obvious that it's Rebekah, not Jacob, who dreams this one up. Jacob wants to back out, afraid he'll get caught, but his mother isn't having any. She has the whole thing planned out, right down to putting the kids' skins on Jacob to make him as hairy as Esau. (This probably gave its original listeners a chuckle. How hairy was Esau? Have you ever seen a baby goat? That's *hairy*. Even Isaac, blind as a bat, knows how hairy Esau is.)

Notice, though, that Isaac asks several times if this is really his son Esau. It's possible that Isaac has his suspicions but is apparently willing to be deceived. Isaac, the Invisible Man, has become Isaac the Unseeing Man. Or perhaps, where his sons were concerned, he always was.

We all know what follows, of course. Esau comes in with his little bowl of game, expecting the blessing, only to discover that it's too late. But note his complaint: "Is he not rightly named Jacob? For he has supplanted me these two times. He took away my birthright; and look, now he has taken away my blessing" (Genesis 27:36). By now Esau has apparently forgotten that he sold his birthright quite happily for a quick lunch. One thing you can say for the Old Testament: its writers knew a dysfunctional family when they saw one.

Esau consoles himself by planning to kill Jacob as soon as Isaac is dead, but again, Rebekah, the managing woman, isn't about to let all her work go to waste. She has a plan for all contingencies. Jacob must go away for a while, and she'll send for him when the coast is clear. She herself goes to Isaac and complains about Esau's Hittite wives in a fairly dramatic style: "I am weary of my life because of the Hittite women. If Jacob marries one of the Hittite women such as these, one of the women of the land, what good will my life be to me?" (Genesis 27:46).

Now read this:

> Then Isaac called Jacob and blessed him, and charged him, "You shall not marry one of the Canaanite women. Go at once to Paddan-aram to the house of Bethuel, your mother's father; and take as wife from there one of the daughters of Laban, your mother's brother. May God Almighty bless you and make you fruitful and numerous, that you may become a company of peoples. May he give to you the blessing of Abraham, to you and to your offspring with you, so that you may take possession of the land where you now live as an alien—land that God gave to Abraham." Thus Isaac sent Jacob away; and he went to Paddan-aram, to Laban son of Bethuel the Aramean, the brother of Rebekah, Jacob's and Esau's mother. (Genesis 28:1–5)

Hello? I recall being given the idea in Sunday School that Esau was within inches of killing Jacob, and so Jacob ran away practically in the middle of the night. But no, in fact, that's not the way it happened. Again, it's Rebekah who has engineered all this, gong to Isaac, knowing that Isaac will do exactly what she wants. Isaac sends Jacob off with his blessing, to make a proper marriage. He's not being forced to flee in the middle of the night: he has the family's commission. (Isaac, you'll note, assumes the boy is capable of picking his own wife.)

Rebekah doesn't believe for one minute that Esau will kill his brother. She knows her son. He burns hot and cold—he'll get all upset, and then something else will come up to take his attention, and he'll forget his anger. Also, Isaac is more than twenty years away from dying here—he probably had a cold and was convinced he was in his last throes. Rebekah doesn't believe he was dying, either. She maneuvers Isaac into thinking he's the one sending Jacob away to find a wife, but Rebekah is in fact managing all of them.

There's a humorous sideline here, too.

> Now Esau saw that Isaac had blessed Jacob and sent him away to Paddan-aram to take a wife from there, and that as he blessed him he charged him, "You shall not marry one of the Canaanite women," and that Jacob had obeyed his father and his mother and gone to Paddan-aram. So when Esau saw that the Canaanite women did not please his father Isaac, Esau went to Ishmael and took Mahalath daughter of Abraham's son Ishmael, and sister of Nebaioth, to be his wife in addition to the wives he had. (Genesis 28:6–9)

Esau may be slow, but he does catch on eventually.

Now let's go back to Rebekah, who isn't the woman we've been told she is. This story is mostly about Rebekah, and how she maneuvers things to get them to come out as she knows they should. What does it say about a woman who tells one son to cheat the other son? Esau, after all, is also her son, her first-born. Granted, he did something very stupid in marrying a pair of women his mother couldn't stand, but there's more here than just that. Esau obviously doesn't understand what God is up to, and doesn't know why a Canaanite isn't God's choice. Isaac, too, seems surprisingly dim, until Rebekah suggests that Jacob needs to marry from within his own kin.

In other words, God's promise is redeemed not because of Isaac or his first-born, but because of the shrewd understanding of Rebekah, and the second-born son, Jacob. It's Rebekah who sets things in motion to insure that the promise will come to pass through a proper line of inheritance, and she's certain that that line doesn't run through Esau. It's sad to reflect that she probably knows she may never see her son Jacob again. Though she's the one who's sending him away, she may never again see him or his wives or children—and there's nothing in the story that indicates she does.

In other words, there's something more at work here than just Rebekah manipulating. True, she *is* manipulating, but it is for a reason, and the reason is probably the exact reason God decided that this would be the young woman who'd come to the well to water the camels.

Isaac is the Invisible Man, a spiritual jellyfish whose God is known as "the Fear of Isaac." Nothing indicates he has a close relationship with God. He simply doesn't understand what's at stake—but Rebekah does. For Isaac, Esau is his first-born son, so he will give him the blessing. But a first-born son who has already married outside the line of blessing? Truly, Isaac *doesn't get* it. Rebekah does. The child of promise, who will pass on the blessing to the next generation, must be born of Abraham's line. Clearly, this isn't Esau, who at the point when the blessing is given, has gone outside his own gene pool and acquired two Hittite wives. The narrator has gone to great lengths to make sure that you know Esau is simply not capable of being trusted with the blessing God gave to Abraham. The textual deck has really been stacked against Esau.

Later on when we see Esau, when Jacob comes back as a patriarch himself, he's an OK guy. There's nothing exactly wrong with him, but by then, of course, the danger has passed. Jacob has already married and begotten the correct progeny to carry the blessing forward. Esau is no longer a threat.

Rebekah isn't a woman who will blindly follow tradition, even though tradition says "the first-born son gets the blessing." Rebekah knows that there's more at stake: the *right* son must get the blessing, or God's plan won't come to pass.

God was never able to get to Isaac, not after their rocky start. But the young woman we see at the well—already breaking tradition in her manner of greeting a stranger—who better than her to see to it that the right son gets the blessing, tradition or no?

As we look at the end of the story, we can see that Esau hasn't really been cheated. He has wives and children, servants and dependents, flocks and herds, and all of his father's property. He's become an important and wealthy man who probably loves being outdoors with the flocks and out hunting with the men. With Jacob gone, Esau gets to be the favorite son with no competition, going out and hunting game for Dad for the next twenty years.

Rebekah, however, has to make a real sacrifice, sending her favorite son off to fulfill his destiny. She does it because she is a woman of substance and character. She knows what this will cost her. But she also knows what's at stake. The one who gets the blessing will be the mediator with God for his people. In her own way, she does what Isaac could not: she places the right son in the position to get the blessing.

True, this is one more instance in which the Ozzie and Harriet family fails to emerge from the pages of Scripture. But Scripture was never intended to extol the Ozzie and Harriet family. The stories we hear are real stories, about real—and fallible—people. They're meant to tell us something enormously important about God. Over and over again God chooses the younger over the older, the weak over the strong. God chooses flawed people. God turns things upside down.

Yes, Isaac the Invisible Man still had the power to pass on the blessing, despite his watery character. And yes, Rebekah played her part in it, despite her flagrant manipulation of those around her. In fact, when you look closely, it looks suspiciously as if an Isaac needs a Rebekah if life is to go on at all.

And Rebekah? I don't think she minded marrying a weak husband at all. A strong one would have been too much to manage.

GRACE'S STORY

My daddy grew up in a very proper, very old-fashioned Southern family, the kind where Grandaddy was the head of the household and his word was more or less law. You could sometimes change his mind, but you never really argued with him. It simply wasn't done. Grandaddy was a doctor, and he had taken over the practice from his daddy, who was a doctor, who had taken over the practice from his daddy, who was also a doctor. You understand, especially in the South, anything you do for three generations is a tradition you wouldn't even dream of breaking! That's how it was with our family.

So as far as Grandaddy was concerned, it was always the family tradition that the oldest son had to become a doctor, which meant that Uncle Lewis, because he was the older son, was going to be a doctor, and my daddy, who was three years younger, was going to work for an uncle who was a watchmaker, because the family had run a jewelry store for one or two generations, too.

My grandmother—and by coincidence, her name was Rebecca, too—she didn't agree at all. She knew who her sons were. She knew perfectly well that Uncle Lewis had always hated school. He wasn't stupid, you understand, he just hated being cooped up indoors and having to study. He was the outdoors type who would rather be out fishing or taking a ride by the river. He absolutely hated the thought of having to go to medical school for all those years, but there was no talking Grandaddy out of it. The eldest son was always a doctor. My daddy, on the other hand, was the brainy one, who had always been the head of his class at school, and would have liked nothing better than the chance to go to medical school. Mechanical things had never interested him much, so he wasn't exactly looking forward to learning watchmaking.

Now, what do you do in a case like this? Grandma was too smart to try arguing with her husband! Southern women have their own way of getting things done, without even getting unpleasant about it. Instead of arguing, she started out by saying things like, "Don't you think Lewis looks a little peaked? He's so pale! I think he's been studying too hard." Now, there was nothing wrong with Lewis. He looked just fine. But if you say something often enough, people will

*start to believe it, and pretty soon, Grandaddy started to agree. So she
kept on, saying, "I'm worried about him, especially if he's going off to
school next year. Do you suppose it would help if we sent him to my
cousin's farm for a few months first? Do you think some fresh country
air would help build up his strength?" Naturally, that appealed to
Grandaddy—after all, he was a doctor.*

*Of course, what Grandma was really thinking was that her
cousin had no son to inherit his farm, but he had three very pretty
daughters, and she knew what young people are like when they're
thrown together every day! So they sent Uncle Lewis off to the farm,
which he absolutely adored. He got to be outdoors all day, and
whenever he came into the house, there were these three beautiful girls
who catered to his every whim and obviously thought he was
wonderful! Well, it doesn't take a genius to figure out what was going
to happen. Within a few months, Uncle Lewis was not only in love
with one of his cousins, but there was already a baby on the way. Ah,
that fresh country air!*

*Naturally, believe me, that took care of medical school. Uncle
Lewis married the girl—country folks were too realistic to consider it
a disgrace—and he raised a nice healthy family, inherited the farm,
and got a life he genuinely loved.*

*Grandma had to do a little more encouraging to see to it that my
daddy was sent to medical school in Uncle Lewis' place when the time
came, but she managed that, too. Grandaddy was a little disappointed
at first, of course, but after a few years, he was so proud of my daddy
being a success as a doctor, you would have thought he had planned it
that way in the first place. In fact, I'm half convinced he thought so, too.*

*I'll admit, Grandma pulled a few strings, but how was that
different from Rebekah in the Bible? Both of those women knew who
their sons were, and who they weren't. They simply helped arrange
things to give their sons the chance to become who they really were,
the way most women try to do with their children. Everyone in the
family gained something when these two women interfered, because
they knew that bending people to fit the tradition doesn't really work.
Sometimes you have to bend the tradition a little instead, so that
people end up with the life that suits them.*

*Men, now, they seem to love tradition so much they sometimes
forget to look at the people who have to live it. Not women. They see
life differently, more realistically. They look at the people first, and the
tradition afterwards. They always have. You'd think by now, we'd
know all this. But it's a lesson they still have to go on teaching people!*

QUESTIONS FOR STUDY AND REFLECTION

In reading the story:
- What do her actions tell us about Rebekah?
- How does she deal with expectations? Customs?
- Is she a good match for Isaac?
- What strengths does she have? What flaws?
- How well does she understand her family?
- How does God "make use" of Rebekah?

Self-reflection and learning:
- Where in my life do I resemble Rebekah? Her family?
- Have I dealt with restrictions and frustrations in similar ways? Different ways?
- What can I learn from her, either good or bad?
- What light does this throw on my own story?

What questions and problems does this still leave unanswered or "in process"?

CHAPTER FIVE

"Sisters, Sisters . . . ": Sibling Rivalry to the Max

"Lord Help the Sister"

Sisters, sisters
There were never such devoted sisters,

. . . . .

Lord help the mister
who comes between me and my sister
And Lord help the sister
who comes between me and my man.[9]

I know. I couldn't resist. It's one of those typical pieces of '50s Hollywood fluff (the kind I soundly disclaimed in the introduction to this book), with a pair of bouncy blonde song-and-dance stars hoofing it up in a country inn (or was this one set in a barn?) to the tune of an Irving Berlin number. Not exactly what you'd associate with Genesis.

The fact is, ever since I started thinking about Rachel and Leah, the song has been dancing around in my head with the maddening insistence of an itch. Whatever the plot of the movie (I think it was *White Christmas*), this song was tailor-made for my favorite exponents of pure sibling rivalry, Rachel and Leah. Granted, it's hard to single out an outstanding example, especially in this family, those wonderful folks who brought you Jacob and Esau, not to mention Joseph and his brothers.

But truly, Rachel and Leah rank as my own personal favorites. For one thing, their story is instructive for a number of reasons, not the least of which is that it 1) disabuses us once and for all of the idea that biblical women were always sweet and agreeable, 2) illustrates how thoroughly we can ignore the actual text in front of our eyes and substitute a purely cultural version of the text, and 3) contains some of the most delicious comedy in Genesis.

It isn't really possible to start their story without harkening back to the incident that precedes their entry into the tale. That is, they enter on the tail-end of Rebekah's plot to secure the blessing for her son Jacob, and his departure for Paddam-Aram, both to get away from Esau until the heat dies down, and to find a wife in the family of Laban, his mother's brother.

Most of us will recall the scene we all heard about in Sunday School, in which, while Jacob was settling down to a rather uncomfortable night's sleep,

> [H]e dreamed that there was a ladder set up on the earth, the top of it reaching to heaven; and the angels of God were ascending and descending on it. And the LORD stood beside him and said, "I am the LORD, the God of Abraham your father and the God of Isaac; the land on which you lie I will give to you and to your offspring; and your offspring shall be like the dust of the earth, and you shall spread abroad to the west and to the east and to the north and to the south; and all the families of the earth shall be blessed in you and in your offspring. Know that I am with you and will keep you wherever you go, and will bring you back to this land; for I will not leave you until I have done what I have promised you." (Genesis 28:12–15)

Notice that the God who's been so silent all during Isaac's story is suddenly back in business again, chatting it up as volubly as he did with his friend Abraham, making promises in almost the identical terms. Obviously, Rebekah knew what she was doing. Jacob has the blessing, he's now the designated one, and God responds by ratifying the agreement he made earlier with Abraham.

In part this is to show us that the blessing really has been passed on to the correct son, and in part it is to underline that Jacob's flight from home is not an unfortunate accident but something that God (with a little help from Rebekah) has especially planned for Jacob. Jacob is so impressed he calls the place of his vision "Bethel," the gate of heaven or the place of God.

But more important, it sounds a note that will lie at the heart of the story that now unfolds: it centers on offspring, offspring more numerous than the grains of dust, offspring that will eventually receive the Promised Land.

ANOTHER MEETING AT A WELL

Meetings at wells, as we've already seen, signal betrothals, marriages, and offspring, as we found in Hagar's two encounters in the wilderness, and Rebekah's first appearance in the story. So when Jacob arrives at his destination and finds a group of shepherds gathered around a well, we might guess that something's about to happen. He immediately asks them if they know Laban, and naturally they not only know Laban, but add ". . . and here is his daughter Rachel, coming with the sheep" (Genesis 29:6).

Then follows an interesting little passage. Jacob tells the shepherds, "Look, it is still broad daylight; it is not time for the animals to be gathered together. Water the sheep, and go, pasture them" (Genesis 29:7). They protest that they have to wait until all the sheep are gathered before they take the stone off the mouth of the well. Why, we may ask, is Jacob, a stranger, suddenly so interested in how the shepherds are tending to the flock? It sounds almost as if he's trying to get rid of them. And when we arrive at the next verse, it becomes clear why.

> *While he was still speaking with them, Rachel came with her father's sheep; for she kept them. Now when Jacob saw Rachel, the daughter of his mother's brother Laban, and the sheep of his mother's brother Laban, Jacob went up and rolled the stone from the well's mouth, and watered the flock of his mother's brother Laban. (Genesis 29:9–10)*

Some families run true to type. Rebekah, when the right messenger came along, lost no time in fetching enough water to satisfy ten camels. Jacob, faced with his newfound cousin, is equally speedy in leaping in to provide water for the flocks. There's something almost laughable in Jacob's eagerness to impress his cousin.

But there's more here, when we stop to look at it. Rachel arrives at the well in charge of her father's sheep, not a task girls of marriageable age usually performed, at least not alone. True, Moses encounters the daughters of Reuel while they're watering their father's sheep in Exodus 2:15–21, even driving off the rival shepherds to help them, but they're in a group and it's clear that Reuel has no sons to perform this task. Rachel is obviously in charge of the flock, a major responsibility when you consider how much a part of the family wealth flocks were. As we'll discover later, she has a number of brothers who could perform this work just as well (Genesis 31:1). And unlike Reuel's daughters, Rachel isn't at all put out by the presence of her fellow-shepherds. She brings the sheep on as if she were simply one of the guys. Shepherds, after all, have to be sturdy enough to extricate sheep from bushes and fight off predators (as we're told in the story of David). Forget Little Bo Peep; Jacob must have seen a young woman with a healthy tan, a free stride, and an air of confidence about her. We may start to guess that this is a young woman who takes after her Aunt Rebekah a bit, or possibly that this is a family where women (at least some of them) act with unusual freedom.

Notice one more thing before we move on. *Leah isn't here.* Just Rachel.

In any event, we soon get to the punch line: "Then Jacob kissed Rachel, and wept aloud. And Jacob told Rachel that he was her father's kinsman, and that he was Rebekah's son; and she ran and told her father" (Genesis 29:11–12).

This is a culture in which strange men don't go around kissing unmarried women, though of course there's the fact that Jacob can claim kinship. But it's not the kinship of a brother or father, who may embrace a sister or daughter without reproach: a cousin is considered the ideal marriage partner in this culture, and the public kiss would have had folks' eyebrows raised right up past their hairlines. But he doesn't simply kiss her: he also weeps. Surely not what one would expect of a young man of Jacob's age and standing. Was he perhaps sharply reminded of his mother and the comfortable home and family he's left? Possible. More than possible.

For the rest, this scene echoes the one in which Rebekah first meets Abraham's servant and then goes pelting off to tell her family about the meeting. Jacob kisses his cousin and weeps, and even while he's weeping, she goes dashing off to tell her family, *á la* Rebekah.

At Home with Laban

Laban, whom we first met streaking out to the well to greet the wealthy stranger with the gold and the camels, comes dashing out again (does *no one* in this family move slowly?) to greet his nephew as effusively as he did the wealthy stranger. Having seen Laban in action once before, it's difficult to take his enthusiasm seriously. He may not have a plan in mind just now, but it's certain he'll come up with one.

After a month has gone by, and Laban has had a chance to get the measure of his nephew, he's come up with a plan.

> Then Laban said to Jacob, "Because you are my kinsman, should you
> therefore serve me for nothing? Tell me, what shall your wages be?"
> Now Laban had two daughters; the name of the elder was Leah, and
> the name of the younger was Rachel. Leah's eyes were lovely, and
> Rachel was graceful and beautiful. Jacob loved Rachel; so he said,
> "I will serve you seven years for your younger daughter Rachel."
> Laban said, "It is better that I give her to you than that I should give
> her to any other man; stay with me." So Jacob served seven years for
> Rachel, and they seemed to him but a few days because of the love
> he had for her. (Genesis 29:15–20)

Yes, of course, we might have guessed. Laban, the old wheeler-dealer, has just scored. He not only has an acceptable husband for one of his daughters, but he doesn't have to provide a dowry for her, and he will get seven years' worth of free labor. He knew something good was bound to happen the day his sister Rebekah traipsed in wearing ten shekels worth of gold.

A note may be necessary here, about all of this interfamily marriage. It wasn't only acceptable in Jacob's days; it was considered the ideal. Marrying within the family kept both the wealth and the progeny inside the clan. When a woman married outside the family, a dowry generally had to be provided, and her children would be considered part of her husband's family, an important point when you consider that the family was essentially an economic unit, not unlike the old farm family. The more hands, the more work they could perform, and the less chance that they could be taken advantage of by their neighbors.

The patriarch, the head of the clan, was regarded as "owning" all of its members, male, female, adult and child, and Laban is the patriarch here, not Jacob. Much later in the story, when Jacob tries to leave him, Laban cries, ". . . the daughters are my daughters, the children are my children, the flocks are my flocks, and all that you see is mine" (Genesis 31:43).

No wonder Laban is only too happy to agree to give Rachel to Jacob. He's about to become a much wealthier man because of the deal, and Jacob in fact isn't being promised anything but a wife. Period.

SISTERS, SISTERS

All right, the other half of the sisters' duet has finally appeared. "Now Laban had two daughters; the name of the elder was Leah, and the name of the younger was Rachel. Leah's eyes were lovely, and Rachel was graceful and beautiful. Jacob loved Rachel" (Genesis 29:16–18).

And there it is, in just three sentences. There are some interesting things here, though. Hearing the story when I was small, I got the distinct impression that Leah was a real dog, while Rachel was not only gorgeous, but sweet. Well, yes, that's the way the pictures in the Sunday School book showed them. Some translations said Leah had "weak" eyes, and anachronistic as it was, I always pictured her with glasses. At best, I saw her as one of those plain, rangy women with knobby knuckles who were forever hauling baskets of laundry up from the cellar in the days before dryers. Likewise, the pictures in my Sunday School book showed Rachel as decidedly petite and winsome.

Find it in the text if you can. It isn't there. Leah has "soft" eyes or "lovely" eyes, and has so far been modestly withdrawn, as befits a proper young woman. Rachel, as we've seen, is graceful and beautiful, and as athletic as a hopeful for the Olympic soccer team. They might be Jacob and Esau in drag.

It's interesting, of course, that our culture assumes that Leah must be homely, and Rachel beautiful, and *of course* Jacob would love Rachel. It really tells us a great deal about us, but nothing about the text we're reading. There is nothing to indicate that Leah is any less good-looking. The storyteller's comments place before us the fact that Laban had two handsome daughters: one with lovely eyes, and one with grace and beauty. Laban had two beautiful daughters, apparently. But Jacob loved the one he first saw at the well, obviously a destined meeting. Could it possibly be that he loved her because she reminded him of his own mother, her aunt, another woman who was free-spirited and never hesitated to break out of traditional roles? Leah hasn't really appeared at all so far, certainly not as a shepherdess out following the flocks. She hasn't spoken at all, and scriptural narrative places great weight on who speaks and who doesn't.

Leah, in fact, simply sounds like a more traditional woman, out of sight within the family tents, rather than moving about in public, a woman with lovely eyes and a more retiring personality. It is perfectly consistent with the text. As set before us, it sounds more as if the storyteller wants us to know that there are two beautiful sisters: one shy and withdrawn, one free-striding and forthright. And Jacob, the son of an energetic woman, is attracted to the one who reminds him of her.

Whatever the reason, he's truly in love, and he happily serves for seven years in order to marry her.

WHY ARE WE NOT SURPRISED?

Having seen Laban in action by now, we may begin to suspect that all this is too easy. There has to be a catch in it somewhere, and of course there is. Again, if we look at the traditional story, we see Laban's master hand at work in the wedding scene.

> So Laban gathered together all the people of the place, and made a
> feast. But in the evening he took his daughter Leah and brought her
> to Jacob; and he went in to her. (Laban gave his maid Zilpah to his
> daughter Leah to be her maid.) When morning came, it was Leah!
> And Jacob said to Laban, "What is this you have done to me? Did I
> not serve with you for Rachel? Why then have you deceived me?"
> Laban said, "This is not done in our country—giving the younger
> before the firstborn. Complete the week of this one, and we will give
> you the other also in return for serving me another seven years."
> Jacob did so, and completed her week; then Laban gave him his
> daughter Rachel as a wife. (Laban gave his maid Bilhah to his
> daughter Rachel to be her maid.) So Jacob went in to Rachel also,
> and he loved Rachel more than Leah. He served Laban for another
> seven years. (Genesis 29:22–30)

Admit it. There are some tantalizing questions here. Granted, brides were usually veiled in those days, but why on earth doesn't Jacob notice the substitution till morning? Victorian readers would have assumed that they modestly had the lights out, but normally the wedding feast would have been going on full tilt while the bride and groom retired to their tent. Was their wedding night conducted in silence as well as darkness? Did Leah keep her robes and veil on till daylight?

Or—given the way weddings were conducted in those days—did the hearers simply assume that, as per the usual custom, the men of the band tried to get the groom as drunk as possible, thinking it was a roaring good joke if they could get him sozzled enough that he couldn't even make it into the marriage tent without being carried. (Yes, well, I'm a first-generation American who remembers the Hungarian weddings of my childhood. They not only got the groom drunk, but the men in the wedding party often kidnapped him and held him for "ransom," which was usually a bottle of whiskey each.)

My guess is that the original hearers would simply have assumed that Jacob was too drunk to know the difference. Moreover, they would've found it decidedly amusing to think that Laban pulled the same switcheroo on Jacob that Rebekah pulled on Isaac. Was this an old family joke, like twins masquerading as each other? Are we to see Jacob as a man as easily bamboozled as his father?

But there's another question we can't afford not to ask. *Why doesn't Rachel give the show away?* She's no shy violet, any more than her Aunt Rebekah was. She hasn't hesitated to speak or to act in the scenes in which we've seen her. There's no hint that Laban feared he wouldn't get away with it. Nor, for that matter, are we told that Leah was afraid she wouldn't get away with it. In fact, there's something very suggestive about Rachel's silence. Could she possibly have been in on the deception?

Keep in mind that this is a culture where most women didn't expect to be the only wife, and the idea of sexual exclusivity on their husbands' part would simply not have occurred to them. Abraham had plenty of progeny by slaves and concubines, even though it was Sarah, his lawful wife, who was supposed to bear his legitimate heir. To some extent the larger the number of children fathered by her husband, the more prestige a wife had: it meant he was a man of wealth and substance.

Nowhere in the subsequent text do either Leah or Rachel question the fact that they are the wives of the same man. That is the way things simply are in this world. Nothing suggests that Rachel is dismayed by Jacob's marriage to her sister. She's a confident woman; she knows she's loved. It would be surprising if she thought that Leah's marriage to Jacob would deprive her of him. She knows her culture. What's more, she knows her father Laban!

THE NURSERY COMPETITION

And of course Laban has no intention of withholding his second daughter from Jacob. Why should he? He's now secured another seven years' service from Jacob. He doesn't even make him wait until the seven years are up. (For one thing, he too is hoping that both his daughters will begin producing sons as soon as possible; they will add to his stature.) So he bargains with Jacob again, and gives him Rachel at the end of his honeymoon week with Leah (Genesis 29:27–30).

There's nothing the least bit irregular in what's happened. Even Jacob really has little cause for complaint. He's a young man and already has two wives, which marks him as a man of substance, as well. But all is not well, of course, and what the storyteller says next is important:

> When the LORD saw that Leah was unloved, he opened her womb;
> but Rachel was barren. Leah conceived and bore a son, and she
> named him Reuben; for she said, "Because the LORD has looked on
> my affliction; surely now my husband will love me." She conceived
> again and bore a son, and said, "Because the LORD has heard that
> I am hated, he has given me this son also"; and she named him
> Simeon. Again she conceived and bore a son, and said, "Now this
> time my husband will be joined to me, because I have borne him
> three sons"; therefore he was named Levi. She conceived again and
> bore a son, and said, "This time I will praise the LORD"; therefore she
> named him Judah; then she ceased bearing. (Genesis 29:31–35)

In rapid succession, Leah produces four sons, something that would give her tremendous status in this culture. It's not simply her husband's love that's at stake: Leah has taken precedence over her sister in a big way. But Leah is aware that all isn't well in her relationship with Jacob. She feels unloved, even "hated." Each time she gives birth she hopes, to no avail, that Jacob will now love her.

There's something so real—and so heartbreaking—about Leah! How many of us live our lives in those terms, *vis á vis* parents, peers, lovers, spouses, even society itself. "If I were just better looking," or "If I were just smarter," or "If I get this job," or "If I get a doctorate," and so on and on. The fact that the first two sons didn't change her situation doesn't keep her from hoping that a third will do it, or a fourth. She will produce half-a-dozen sons, and it will never be enough. Because the fact is, if you're a Leah in your own mind, nothing is ever enough.

But four sons certainly have significance for Rachel. The young woman who was so confident discovers that there's something she cannot do, she cannot control. She knows who's given respect by her society, and that she is ranked as inferior to her more fertile sister. What she says to Jacob reveals something important.

> When Rachel saw that she bore Jacob no children, she envied her
> sister; and she said to Jacob, "Give me children, or I shall die!" Jacob
> became very angry with Rachel and said, "Am I in the place of God,
> who has withheld from you the fruit of the womb?" (Genesis 30:1–2)

Sarah knows that only God can give her offspring; Rachel doesn't look that high. She accuses Jacob, who knows perfectly well that he isn't God.

Unlike his father, who prayed for his wife's barrenness, Jacob does nothing more. He, after all, already has plenty of progeny, and he seems oddly insensitive to Rachel's need. (Even Hannah's husband, in 1 Samuel 1:4–8, gives her a double portion of the sacrifice, "because he loved her, though the LORD had closed her womb," and asks her, "Am I not more to you than ten sons?")

Unprayed for, and no doubt feeling that she is totally on her own, Rachel, like Sarah before her, takes her maid Bilhah and gives her to Jacob so that she can become a mother through her. And, with no apparent problem, Bilhah promptly gets pregnant and has a son, whom Rachel names Dan, because ". . . God has judged me, and has also heard my voice and given me a son." Bilhah has a second son, whom Rachel names Napthali, because "With mighty wrestlings I have wrestled with my sister, and have prevailed" (Genesis 30:3–8).

How unlike the story of Sarah and Hagar this is. There is no hint that Bilhah is seen as a threat. She doesn't even get to name the two boys; Rachel does. Moreover, Rachel feels satisfied with these results. She has wrestled with mighty wrestlings, and prevailed over her sister.

RAISING THE STAKES

Now that Rachel has entered the maternity stakes, Leah feels the need to retaliate, so she gives her maid Zilpah to Jacob, and the maid promptly gets pregnant. She, too, bears a son, whom Leah names Gad (good fortune). When Zilpah bears a second son, she exclaims, "Happy am I! For the women will call me happy"; so she named him Asher (Genesis 30:9–13).

If it weren't so serious to them, there would be something almost laughable in this maternity competition.

And there's something laughable in the little gem about Leah, Rachel, and the mandrakes Leah's son found (Genesis 30:14–18). Mandrake roots were believed to have aphrodisiac properties, so Rachel, hoping to spark Jacob's interest in her, asks Leah for the mandrakes. Leah responds rather snappishly that, as if it isn't enough that Rachel has taken her husband, now she wants to take her son's mandrakes as well. Rachel strikes a bargain: if Leah will give her the mandrakes, she'll send Jacob to have sex with her sister.

Well, these are, after all, Laban's daughters.

> When Jacob came from the field in the evening, Leah went out to meet him, and said, "You must come in to me; for I have hired you with my son's mandrakes." So he lay with her that night. And God heeded Leah, and she conceived and bore Jacob a fifth son. Leah said, "God has given me my hire because I gave my maid to my husband"; so she named him Issachar. (Genesis 30:16–18)

First, there is something the early hearers must have found terrifically amusing about the picture of Jacob, being yanked from one woman to another. For a patriarchal society, in which he was supposed to own his wives as sexual property, this picture of family life is rather delicious, and real-life families of that era would no doubt have gotten the joke. Jacob has to satisfy four women, and after a hard day's work, he's told that it's Leah's turn, and that moreover, in case he tries to beg off by saying he has a headache, she's hired him for the night. And Jacob apparently knows better than to protest.

Leah has a sixth son, and finally, a daughter named Dinah.

If you've been keeping score (or if you've lost track of it), the count now stands at Leah, 6; Bilhah, 2; Zilpah, 2; and Rachel, 0. Jacob has ten sons, which is a more than respectable number. Oh. And a daughter.

Now, at long last,

> Then God remembered Rachel, and God heeded her and opened her womb. She conceived and bore a son, and said, 'God has taken away my reproach'; and she named him Joseph, saying, "May the LORD add to me another son!" (Genesis 30:22–24)

Whew!

ANOTHER BIRTHING COMPETITION

By this time we may feel as if we've come through one of the greatest birthing competitions of all time, but there's one more. This, in Genesis 30:25–43, is another glimpse of Laban's craftiness, and Jacob's growing skill in outwitting his father-in-law. Jacob decides the time has come to go home. (Surely Esau must have cooled off by now! It's been nearly twenty years since Jacob left home.) Laban, of course, doesn't want to let go of Jacob, since the flocks Jacob has tended and increased, not to mention all the healthy boy babies Jacob has fathered, are accounted as Laban's. If Jacob goes, Laban will be a considerably poorer man.

So they bargain over the correct wages for Jacob, and at length Jacob says he'll take the spotted, speckled, and black animals of the flock. Laban agrees, and then, before they can make a reckoning, removes all the speckled, spotted, and black sheep and goats and sends them out of the main flock. He may be sharp, but he's no hero, so Laban, "[S]et a distance of three days' journey between himself and Jacob, while Jacob was pasturing the rest of Laban's flock" (Genesis 30:36).

Not to be outdone, Jacob places wands that have been peeled in spots and stripes in front the animals when they breed, so that their offspring will be spotted and speckled. Pretty soon he has more than enough spotted, speckled, and black sheep and goats to make him a wealthy man.

Interestingly enough, when Jacob recounts the contest with Laban to his wives, he attributes everything he did to God's guidance, a thing not hinted at in the story itself (Genesis 31:1–13). It's possible he wonders about whether their loyalty will be to him, or to their father. But for once, Leah and Rachel are in agreement.

> Then Rachel and Leah answered him, "Is there any portion or inheritance left to us in our father's house? Are we not regarded by him as foreigners? For he has sold us, and he has been using up the money given for us. All the property that God has taken away from our father belongs to us and to our children; now then, do whatever God has said to you." (Genesis 31:14–16)

After all these years, they are as one. They'll stand by their man, both of them. All four of them. All sixteen of them. For good measure, Rachel waits until her father has gone to see to his own sheep, and then steals the household gods (Genesis 31:19). Yes, gods. The Hebrews are not yet monotheists. There's a special relationship between Abraham, Isaac, Jacob, and one particular God, but there's no hint that they don't believe in other gods, or that other members of the family don't worship other gods. Rachel, knowing that she'll be leaving the ancestral home behind, is taking no chances. She'll kidnap the little statues of the family gods and take them with her into the new country she's about to enter. People need all the divine help they can get.

THE PARTING OF THE WAYS

Laban, like a great many swindlers, gets really angry when somebody outfoxes him. He goes in pursuit of Jacob, but prudently decides that a real confrontation isn't smart (Genesis 31:22–35).

In a performance that is pure ham, Laban all but turns on the waterworks, demanding, "'What have you done? You have deceived me and carried away my daughters like captives of the sword. Why did you flee secretly and deceive me and not tell me? I would have sent you away with mirth and songs, with tambourine and lyre. And why did you not permit me to kiss my sons and my daughters farewell?'" But eventually he gets to the real point: "[W]hy did you steal my gods?"

In the biblical equivalent of "So search me!" Jacob demands that Laban look anywhere in the encampment. Rachel hides the gods in a camel saddle and perches on it, coolly telling Dad that she's having her period, and knowing perfectly well that renders her so unclean no self-respecting man would even come near her. (Even if Rachel weren't a source of major pollution at that moment, later generations of hearers no doubt thought it was vastly amusing to think of the gods hidden in a smelly camel saddle, with Rachel's rump planted firmly on them. So much for those foreign idols!)

Jacob and Laban are not the only sharpies in this family. It begins to look like a genetic trait.

THE DEATH OF A RIVALRY

Sad to say, we see little more of Leah and Rachel from this point in the story. The focus shifts back to Jacob and Esau. On a poignant note, it's Rachel who ends the birthing competition, by giving birth to a final son while they're journeying from Bethel to Ephrath.

> When she was in her hard labor, the midwife said to her, "Do not be
> afraid; for now you will have another son." As her soul was departing
> (for she died), she named him Ben-oni; but his father called him
> Benjamin.[10] So Rachel died, and she was buried on the way to
> Ephrath (that is, Bethlehem), and Jacob set up a pillar at her grave;
> it is the pillar of Rachel's tomb, which is there to this day.
> (Genesis 35:17–20)

There's a final little irony in the contest between the sisters. When Jacob is on the point of death, years later, he tells his sons,

> "I am about to be gathered to my people. Bury me with my
> ancestors—in the cave in the field of Ephron the Hittite, in the cave
> in the field at Machpelah, near Mamre, in the land of Canaan, in the
> field that Abraham bought from Ephron the Hittite as a burial site.
> There Abraham and his wife Sarah were buried; there Isaac and his
> wife Rebekah were buried; and there I buried Leah—the field and the
> cave that is in it were purchased from the Hittites."
> (Genesis 49:29–32)

After all the conflict and all the rivalry, Rachel's grave will lie far away from the ancestral home, while Leah gets to sleep with Jacob for all eternity. And the rivalry doesn't really end with the death of the sisters: their children play it out on an even higher scale, when Rachel's first-born, Joseph, is sold into slavery by his jealous brothers.

Ah, sibling rivalry! Some families make a positive tradition of it.

At the end of their story, we're left wondering if, with her rival gone, Leah was finally content with her husband, but the Scriptures are silent on the point. What we're left with is the picture of two women, each strong and determined in a different way, struggling for what they wanted most, two women who probably never understood what they'd achieved in the first place.

It was, after all, Joseph, Rachel's firstborn, who saved the Israelites from famine and war, indirectly, the cause of their being in Egypt when God sent

Moses to deliver them. His is one of the most riveting stories in Genesis, but his was not the line that dominated Israel's history.

It was Leah who "won" in the end, who became the ancestress of kings (King David descends from her fourth son, Judah), and finally the ancestress of Jesus.

Here indeed is "strife closed in the sod,"[11] a struggle that obsessed two women during their lifetime, and even carried over to their children, but whose results were a boundless blessing for those who came long after. The promise of offspring as numerous as the stars in the sky, or the grains of dust in the world, was fulfilled for their children, if not for them.

It's a powerful reminder that we, ourselves, will never know the ends of our own stories.

NANCY'S STORY

By now I should be an expert on sibling rivalry. I've had lots of practice telling my story to therapists. And I'm good at telling stories. But even I couldn't have dreamed up the ending to this one. Only God could have done that.

My sister Catherine and I were born barely a year apart, as if Mom wanted to get pregnant as quickly as she could. Which is exactly what she wanted. She and Dad had lost a five-year-old son to polio several years before Catherine was born, and I think they were hoping they'd have another son. Unfortunately, they got Catherine instead. As if that weren't bad enough, I came along a year later. And a few months after that, Mom had to have a hysterectomy. So much for having another son.

Dad responded by withdrawing into his work, but Mom just sort of faded, like a human version of the Cheshire Cat. She dressed beautifully, she smiled graciously, she walked like a fashion model, she smelled divine—and she was loaded with enough tranquilizers to knock the entire population of Detroit out for a month and a half. She got pneumonia when I was six, and she just faded out for good.

So then it was just Catherine and me, and of course Dad. Talk about dysfunctional families: a man who was totally absorbed in his work, and two clueless little girls who wanted so desperately to prove to themselves that he loved them. And of course nothing we could do proved anything at all.

Catherine was the beautiful one, who looked exactly like our mother. She had that very fair skin that looks like porcelain, and these enormous blue eyes, complete with eyelashes that the rest of us would kill for. She was one of those people who could look cool on the hottest days and could have put on a flour sack and made it look like a Dior original. I, on the other hand, could take a shower, put on a fresh outfit, and within ten minutes I'd look like I'd been dragged through a Turkish bath. Her socks never fell down. Mine never stayed up. No hint of acne ever threatened her complexion. I was the Clearasil Queen of Coolidge High.

I, on the other hand, got Dad's brains. Since I knew by the time I was ten that I wasn't going to make it on looks, I concentrated on shooting for a Nobel Prize. And so it went on. Catherine got chosen as Homecoming Queen. I got elected to the National Honor Society. She became a cheerleader. I became the President of the Debating Society. She went steady with Harley the Hunk, Captain of the Football Team. I spent evenings with Nelson the Nerd, working on a science project that actually won us a national award.

Catherine married a guy whose father owned half of downtown. I got a scholarship to Stanford. Catherine's husband built her a vacation home in Aspen. I got an M.A. Catherine became a congressional wife. I got my doctorate. It was the world's most complicated tennis game you ever saw. Ball in your court? Dine at the White House. Ball in my court? Publish a book.

When you look at it, it's about the most insane thing you could imagine. Two sisters, just a year apart, and we never communicated: we just sent each other what amounted to press releases. "Oh, and by the way, did I tell you that I . . . blah blah blah."

Of course, even super achievers can only achieve so much. Her marriage fell apart. I got busted for possession. She married a guy who beat her up and disappeared. I woke up in detox. We glossed over these lapses, pulled ourselves together, and went on. Denial can be one hell of a survival tool.

Until—what is it they say about coincidence? That it's God's way of maintaining anonymity? Dad was dying of cancer, and so we both had to go back home to see him. We hung around the hospital, still telling each other how great our lives were, but it was a real strain. About the third evening I was there I just had to get away to an A.A. meeting, so I told her some lie or another and took off. I got lost looking for the meeting, so I got there late, and took a seat way in the back near the door. And all of a sudden I realized I was looking at the rear view of a woman who had just stood up and was saying, "Hi, my name is Catherine, and I'm an alcoholic."

No, you wouldn't believe it if it happened to you. I didn't believe it and it did happen to me. We spent most of that night crying on each other's shoulders and laughing like maniacs, as if we couldn't get the truth out fast enough. We had waited so long to tell the truth!

I never knew how much she envied me. She never knew how much I envied her. We neither of us realized until we were in our forties that we had never actually seen Dad sober, he kept the tank topped off with martinis so successfully. She could have become Miss America, and I really could have won the Nobel Prize, and he would never have noticed anyway.

So much for sibling rivalry.

Happy ending? I don't know. Catherine is trying to make her third marriage work. I'm staying sober one day at a time. But we have each acquired a sister—a real sister, not a competitor—for the first time. God has an odd sense of timing, but I think this was the right time for both of us. Catherine has become a sister worth having. Come to think of it, so have I.

QUESTIONS FOR STUDY AND REFLECTION

In reading the story:

- What does the narrative tell us about the sisters' personalities?
- What does their relationship tell us?
- Who "wins" the competition? Who "loses"?
- How do they involve others in their story?
- Where are they by the end of the story?

Self-reflection and learning:

- Have I been part of a Leah-and-Rachel competition in my life?
- Who do I identify with more: Leah or Rachel?
- Where in my life have I been like them?
- Have I been able to do things differently than they did?

What questions and problems does this still leave unanswered or "in process"?

CHAPTER SIX

Ruth and Naomi:
"Getting by with a Little Help from Our Friends"

AN EVERYDAY STORY

Unlike all the women we've seen so far, Ruth and Naomi actually get a book of their own, a story that doesn't simply weave in and out of other, larger and more impressive themes. It's a tidy little story, really, the kind they used to encourage you to write in English class. It has a beginning, a middle, and an ending. There are no moral ambiguities or theological subtleties here, as we've had to struggle with in dealing with Hagar and Sarah, or Rebekah. It's a *story*. And whoever told this story originally knew how to tell a story: get in there and keep it moving. This is the veritable paperback of biblical stories, though it's not exactly a Harlequin Romance. (Though countless retellers have tried to turn it into that, as we'll also see.)

The interesting thing, of course, is that Ruth and Naomi not only have a book all their own, but that it has been so lovingly preserved down through all the generations, when quite important chunks of chronicle and history have simply disappeared over time. Granted, we more or less expect to have the accounts of Abraham and Isaac, Jacob and Moses preserved. But think about it a moment: this is a story about two widows, not even *important* widows. They're poor widows living on the equivalent of welfare during part of their saga. They have no power, no interesting revelations from God. In fact, God doesn't appear at all in this story, except to be referred to by the characters in the most ordinary fashion—the folks who talk about God aren't prophets or seers but ordinary people commenting on what God seems to be up to. God doesn't appear in visions; God doesn't say weighty things. God doesn't send an angel as a surrogate, or even offer these women a portentous dream.

No, what we have is just an everyday kind of story about two relatively unimportant little figures, the sort whose stories exist all around us all the time without us noticing very much at all. But someone has always thought the story is important enough to be given its place up among the weightier tomes. It's important enough that it's the scroll read on Shavuot, the Jewish festival with roots in the old harvest festival at which the first fruits were dedicated, and which also celebrates the giving of the Torah, the priceless gift of the Law. Quite an important position for a pair of welfare widows to occupy, particularly when you stop to reflect that one of them was a foreigner to begin with!

And yet, even as a story read on an important festival, its earthy roots remain clearly visible. It is, hands down, one of the most down-to-earth, slyest, and most deliciously funny stories in the entire Old Testament. A story told by people who knew very well that God has always had a keen sense of humor.

BEGINNING AT THE BEGINNING

With this much said, we find ourselves as the story opens in a scene not all that unfamiliar from what we've already seen with Abraham, Isaac, and the children of Jacob. In fact, it begins with a descendent of Jacob's line, a man who lives in Bethlehem (which is where Rachel was buried).

> *In the days when the judges ruled, there was a famine in the land,*
> *and a certain man of Bethlehem in Judah went to live in the country*
> *of Moab, he and his wife and two sons. The name of the man was*
> *Elimelech and the name of his wife Naomi, and the names of his two*
> *sons were Mahlon and Chilion; they were Ephrathites from*
> *Bethlehem in Judah. They went into the country of Moab and*
> *remained there. (Ruth 1:1–2)*

Moving from one location to another when famine came was often the lot of people whose lives were either unsettled, as with nomads and traders, or marginal, as with subsistence farmers. The idea was that you went where there was food, and with great good luck, you might survive to come back again. We really aren't told of Elimelech's state in life, but he's named his sons Mahlon ("Sickly") and Chilion ("Frail"). Not your basic optimist, obviously. He certainly thought he'd be better off in Moab, and that would have told the early hearers something. The biblical writers didn't admire Moab—Moabites were Canaanites, and more than once they were The Chief Enemy of Israel. Moreover, they worshiped gods who were highly offensive to the prophets.

Far from being as harmless as it sounds, going to live among the Moabites would have been a bit like defecting to the U.S.S.R. during the Cold War. Respectable folks would rather have starved at home. Listeners to the original story, in fact, might not have been too surprised at what follows:

> *But Elimelech, the husband of Naomi, died, and she was left with her*
> *two sons. These took Moabite wives; the name of the one was Orpah*
> *and the name of the other Ruth. When they had lived there about ten*
> *years, both Mahlon and Chilion also died, so that the woman was left*
> *without her two sons and her husband. (Ruth 1:3–5)*

Maybe Mahlon and Chilion were well named after all. But you can almost see people nodding their heads emphatically at this passage. That's what comes of going off to live with the Moabites. And to let your sons marry Moabite wives! No good ever came of that, did it?

Which is where some of the main surprise lies in this story. Yes, Ruth is a Moabite, a foreigner, not a woman of Israel at all, a Canaanite woman whose people worship strange gods.

Naomi is really in the soup now, a widow with no sons and nothing but a pair of Moabite daughters-in-law. As we have seen earlier, widows were the true unfortunates of Israel's society. A woman without a husband or a son to act for her was a woman largely without power. In this case, she wasn't only without power, but we can assume that she had no claim to either property or wealth. They'd fled to Moab to escape hardship; now Naomi finds herself in even more hardship. She doesn't even have a family to whom she can turn for help. She's an alien in a foreign community.

This, at least, can be remedied. Naomi decides to return to Bethlehem.

> . . . . *[F]or she had heard in the country of Moab that the* LORD *had*
> *considered his people and given them food. So she set out from the*
> *place where she had been living, she and her two daughters-in-law,*
> *and they went on their way to go back to the land of Judah. But*
> *Naomi said to her two daughters-in-law, "Go back each of you to*
> *your mother's house. May the* LORD *deal kindly with you, as you have*
> *dealt with the dead and with me. The* LORD *grant that you may find*
> *security, each of you in the house of your husband." Then she kissed*
> *them, and they wept aloud. (Ruth 1:6–9)*

This begins to flesh out the personalities of Ruth and Naomi for us. As devastated as she must be with her own losses, Naomi is genuinely concerned for her daughters-in-law, referring to their kindness to her dead sons and to herself. Obviously there is affection and gratitude here, but Naomi recognizes that she can't offer her daughters-in-law any security. Each must return to her "mother's house," as honorable widows who would naturally be taken into the women's quarters and provided for by their birth families.

They protest at first, preferring to remain with Naomi rather than go back to their families. (When we stop to think about it they are, after all, Moabite women who are the widows of foreigners—poor foreigners at that.

They won't be considered very desirable on the marriage market in Moab.)

Naomi, however, points out that she has no more sons for them to marry and isn't likely to give birth to any more. In the Levirate law of Israel, if a man died without having fathered a son, his next-of-kin, usually his brother, had to marry the widow and try to get her pregnant. That first son wouldn't be considered his heir, but the heir of the dead kinsman. It was a way of keeping the dead man's property intact, as well as providing security for women without children.

Finally, she says,

> "Even if I thought there was hope for me, even if I should have a husband tonight and bear sons, would you then wait until they were grown? Would you then refrain from marrying? No, my daughters, it has been far more bitter for me than for you, because the hand of the LORD has turned against me." Then they wept aloud again. Orpah kissed her mother-in-law, but Ruth clung to her. (Ruth 1:12–14)

Naomi is certain, now, that God has truly abandoned her; her life is over. Orpah, the more practical of the two daughters-in-law, goes home, but Ruth refuses, as if determined to share the lot of the woman who considers herself scorned by God.

In one of the most often-quoted passages in Scripture, Ruth says:

> "Do not press me to leave you
> or to turn back from following you!
> Where you go, I will go;
> Where you lodge, I will lodge;
> your people shall be my people,
> and your God my God.
> Where you die, I will die—
> there will I be buried.
> May the LORD do thus and so to me,
> and more as well,
> if even death parts me from you!" (Ruth 1:16–17)

Oddly enough, it's a reading that's very popular at weddings, though it has nothing to do with marriage, and in fact, is from a scene played out by two destitute widows who have no future to look forward to. The object of Ruth's tender devotion is not a bridegroom, but her mother-in-law, a woman past childbearing age. Makes you wonder how many wedding planners have actually read the Bible!

The fact is, as a declaration of devotion, it's even more touching than the sentimental misreading it's given at weddings. Ruth has nothing to gain by going with Naomi; she has everything to lose, especially when we hear the line: "your people shall be my people, and your God my God."

Here's one of the truly astonishing pieces of the story. Gods in the culture of Israel and Canaan in the time in which the story is set are *particular*, not universal. The gods of each city look after the people of that city. The gods of Moab have no interest in the people of Egypt. The gods whose images are tended to by each family (as we saw with Laban's household gods) care for the members of that family. To abandon one's gods is a truly terrifying prospect, since if you leave your own gods, there are simply no other gods who are obliged to look after you. Ruth is offering to part with far more than the security of returning to her own family. She's turning her back forever on the only gods on whom she really has any claim. This is an act of almost awesome trust! Giving up her people for Naomi's people actually pales beside it.

Why? Why does she make this absolutely extraordinary offer?

MAKING A FAMILY, MAKING A PEOPLE

Since nothing in the passage implies that Ruth is without a family, it sounds peculiarly as if she simply prefers to stay with Naomi, and a relatively insecure future, to going back to the relative security of her family. While the ancient world (and the modern one, for that matter), assumed that the family would be the ultimate provider, whether of love, security, or physical care, it doesn't always work out that way.

Hallmark Greetings aside, there are some mothers who don't fill you with a warm cozy glow, and some who would make a constipated rhino look like a paragon of loving kindness in comparison. There are some families out there who would make the best of us volunteer for orphanhood. Even in less drastic terms, the families we're born into aren't always the families we need, even with the best of intentions on both sides.

There are many of us who discover early on that, even if we love our families dearly, we cannot live in the same world with them. We don't speak their language, or we don't share their values, or we don't find in them the answers to our needs. And thanks be to God, many of us discover that families don't have to consist merely of the people you are born to; they can also consist of the people you gather into your life, the ones you can talk to, share with, and turn to for acceptance, no strings attached.

These are the families that families are supposed to be, and while the greeting card folks wouldn't approve, God is the ultimate realist when it comes to this point. A family is made as much as born; so are a people. And this, in fact, is one of the reasons why the modest little book of Ruth has managed to survive in the midst of the more impressive scrolls: it sounds the theme that is sounded over and over again in Scripture. *God is always reaching out to gather in a people.*

God calls Abraham and his progeny in order to make a people; God goes into Egypt to bring out a collection of slaves and foreigners and make them a people; in the New Testament world, God drags in a ragtag collection of Jews, Gentiles, tax collectors, prostitutes, and just plain oddballs and makes them a people. That's the way God always works.

Ruth and Naomi are one little glimpse of this process at work. God will start with a destitute widow staying in a foreign land and her foreign daughter-in-law, and they will form a nucleus out of which a real family will grow. And out of that, a people will be made great.

But the making of families, or people, takes quite a bit of doing, and Ruth and Naomi have just begun their journey.

> When Naomi saw that she was determined to go with her, she said no more to her. So the two of them went on until they came to Bethlehem." (Ruth 1:18–19)

One last word on this: these two women are undertaking a very serious journey. To get back to Bethlehem from Moab, which is in Judea, they will have to go all the way around the Dead Sea and through some of the most inhospitable geography in the Holy Land. Moreover, as poor women, they'll have to go on foot, since camels and donkeys are expensive. The roads are unpaved (where they are anything more than donkey-tracks), and there will be few places to stay. This is a journey of weeks or even months, and it will not only be difficult, but unsafe. Most travelers try to go with a band of other people who are heading in the same general direction; attaching oneself to a trading group, for instance. The one advantage Ruth and Naomi have is that they probably aren't worth robbing. We don't really see the details of their journey, but the original hearers must have had a good idea of how difficult it was.

BACK HOME AGAIN

They must have looked fairly grungy by the time they arrived in Bethlehem, where of course Naomi's old neighbors greeted them:

> So the two of them went on until they came to Bethlehem. When they came to Bethlehem, the whole town was stirred because of them; and the women said, "Is this Naomi?" (Ruth 1:19)

In other words, "Well, look who's back! Naomi? I wouldn't have recognized her!"

Small towns are like that. Keep in mind that going off to Moab when things got tough in Bethlehem would not have been the most popular move in the eyes of the neighbors. The family that went off so confident of finding a better life in Moab, the family that consisted of three men and a woman, comes back stripped of everything, consisting of one travel-worn widow and a foreigner, an outsider, a woman of no family at all. For Naomi, who had gone off a respectable wife and the mother of sons, it must have been the ultimate admission of failure.

> *She said to them,*
> *"Call me no longer Naomi ["Pleasant"],*
> *call me Mara ["Bitter"],*
> *for the Almighty has dealt bitterly with me.*
> *I went away full,*
> *but the LORD has brought me back empty;*
> *why call me Naomi*
> *when the LORD has dealt harshly with me,*
> *and the Almighty has brought calamity upon me?"*
> *(Ruth 1:20–21)*

Naomi is merely echoing the conventional religious views of her times: prosperity and hardship alike are attributed to God. The prosperous are obviously good folks, because you can see how much God loves them. The poor are obviously not in God's good books, or why would they be poor? Come to think of it, the conventional wisdom of the ancient Middle East is alive and well and living in Grand Rapids, Austin, and Los Angeles. Naomi (and her neighbors, no doubt) is certain that God is behind the calamity.

> *So Naomi returned together with Ruth the Moabite, her daughter-in-*
> *law, who came back with her from the country of Moab. They came*
> *to Bethlehem at the beginning of the barley harvest. (Ruth 1:22)*

Ironically, she's arrived at the time when the rest of Bethlehem will be celebrating their fullness, their increased wealth, accompanied by a Moabite woman, a foreigner, as the storyteller loses no opportunity to remind us.

But harvest time, as bitter as it may seem to Naomi, is about to change everything.

> *Now Naomi had a kinsman on her husband's side, a prominent rich*
> *man, of the family of Elimelech, whose name was Boaz. And Ruth the*
> *Moabite said to Naomi, "Let me go to the field and glean among the*
> *ears of grain, behind someone in whose sight I may find favor." She*
> *said to her, "Go, my daughter." So she went. She came and gleaned in*
> *the field behind the reapers. As it happened, she came to the part of*
> *the field belonging to Boaz, who was of the family of Elimelech.*
> *(Ruth 2:1–3)*

Ah, sounds like the storyteller is setting something up. First she tosses in a rich relative, of whom we haven't heard before, then she moves on immediately to the mundane little scene of Ruth offering to go out and glean in the fields.

There's more in this tiny scene than is obvious. First, gleaning behind the reapers is a form of welfare not only practiced by the Hebrews, but absolutely commanded by God. At harvest time, the fields can't be harvested all the way to their margins: a border must be left uncut for widows and orphans to come and harvest. Moreover, if the reapers drop anything, they're not allowed to retrieve it. That, too, must be left for the gleaners. To go into the fields to glean is to make a public admission of neediness, an admission that automatically relegates you to the lowest social status (as if you weren't already there). Ruth isn't simply offering to do some tough, backbreaking work; she is, in effect, actually offering to spare Naomi's pride. She, Ruth, will be the public object of the community's charity.

On the other hand, consider the other part of her statement: "Let me go to the field and glean among the ears of grain, behind someone in whose sight I may find favor." Ruth isn't exactly dense. She is a younger and no doubt more attractive woman than Naomi, and if you're going to go out and ask for charity, that never hurts. And, as we'll see, she gets that one right!

Love Among the Barley Stalks

> *So she went. She came and gleaned in the field behind the reapers. As it happened, she came to the part of the field belonging to Boaz, who was of the family of Elimelech. Just then Boaz came from Bethlehem. He said to the reapers, "The LORD be with you." They answered, "The LORD bless you." Then Boaz said to his servant who was in charge of the reapers, "To whom does this young woman belong?" (Ruth 2:3–5)*

This has been a popular theme in art for centuries: Ruth, the winsome foreigner, among the harvesters, radiating goodness and virtue, and catching the benign (and equally virtuous) eye of Boaz. Yes, right. Have you ever harvested anything? I mean, let's get real here. This is hot, sweaty work, and far from looking winsome, after twenty minutes you look like something that's been dragged in off the compost heap. By the end of the day, you smell like it, too.

On the other hand, I recall seeing one grand Victorian canvas on the theme that came laughably close to what the original hearers would have pictured. Here is Boaz, mounted on an impressive-looking steed, gazing down at the rear elevation of a young woman bending over to pick up the grain. It's a very attractive rear end, too. But of course, no Victorian would object to having this print in his parlor because after all, it was a *religious* painting. Wasn't it?

Point taken. Country people tend to be a lot more realistic than Victorian ladies and gents, and bucolic humor is very earthy. The young men who worked the fields were definitely aware of the relative physical charms of the young women whose derriéres they had a chance to observe to every advantage during the harvest day. Of course she catches Boaz's eye. She's a young, attractive woman, and moreover, one he doesn't know. But notice the way he inquires about her: "To whom does this young woman belong?"

This is *the* important question in ancient Israel, or in much of the world today, in fact. "Who are you?" means "Who are your relatives?" or "Who are your people?" In the biblical culture, this was especially true of women. A man might be identified by his town, his trade, or some notable thing he'd done: we see all of those in Scripture. But a woman is always identified by her male relatives, usually her father or husband.

> *The servant who was in charge of the reapers answered, "She is the Moabite who came back with Naomi from the country of Moab. She said, 'Please, let me glean and gather among the sheaves behind the reapers.' So she came, and she has been on her feet from early this morning until now, without resting even for a moment."*
> *(Ruth 2:6–7)*

Interestingly, the young man's answer underlines Ruth's foreignness: she is "the Moabite who came back with Naomi," not "Naomi's daughter-in-law." He is saying, in effect, "She's not one of us. She's that foreign woman." However, he assures his boss that she observed the proper form for getting permission to glean and has been a hard worker.

> *Then Boaz said to Ruth, "Now listen, my daughter, do not go to glean in another field or leave this one, but keep close to my young women. Keep your eyes on the field that is being reaped, and follow behind them. I have ordered the young men not to bother you. If you get thirsty, go to the vessels and drink from what the young men have drawn." (Ruth 2:8–9)*

Aha! Boaz obviously likes what Ruth adds to the scenery and wants to make sure she sticks around. He even orders the young men not to bother her (which might be a way of telling them not to get too friendly because he himself intends to get friendly). But on another level, there is that phrase "my daughter." Now, granted, in many cultures, using kinship terms is an everyday courtesy. Addressing an older person as "Grandpa" or "Auntie" is courteous, in an informal sort of way; calling someone "Brother" or "Cousin" implies friendliness, not necessarily blood relationship. But here Boaz has addressed a foreigner, a Moabite, as "daughter," and that isn't usual at all. It's one thing for Naomi, her mother-in-law, to call her "daughter." But here is a wealthy man, a property owner, speaking to a foreign gleaner as "daughter." This is a gesture of gathering in, which is, after all, one of the themes of this story.

Ruth, too, is well aware of how unusual Boaz's graciousness is. She falls down at his feet and asks, "Why have I found favor in your sight, that you should take notice of me, when I am a foreigner?" (Ruth 2:10). Boaz replies that he has heard how good she has been to Naomi and adds, ". . . . you left your father and mother and your native land and came to a people that you did not know before. May the LORD reward you for your deeds, and may you have a full reward from the LORD, the God of Israel, under whose wings you have come for refuge!" (Ruth 2:11–12).

Boaz, too, recognizes what Ruth has given up to come to a foreign land with Naomi and invokes a blessing from God, "under whose wings you have come for refuge." From this point on, Boaz will take it upon himself to be one of the channels through which God will, in turn, bless Ruth for her care of Naomi. At lunchtime, he invites her over to eat with his own paid harvest workers (not a usual gleaner's right), and heaps up enough lunch on her plate that she can't possibly stuff it all in, and has some left over to take home for supper. Moreover, he instructs the reapers to deliberately drop some extra grain so she'll have more to glean. She finishes out the day with quite a haul to take home to Naomi (Ruth 2:14–17).

Oh, yes, indeed. Ruth has made a big-time hit with Boaz, and the storyteller, who is extremely good at this, moves effortlessly back and forth between the serious and the light: yes, Boaz is being unusually charitable, because he is a good and pious man. But yes, Boaz is being a great deal more charitable than he would be if this was his elderly relative Naomi instead of this young Moabite woman.

A LITTLE HELP FROM OUR FRIENDS

That night, when Ruth tells Naomi that the man whose fields she worked in was Boaz, Naomi is positively electrified. Listen to her reply: "Blessed be he by the LORD, whose kindness has not forsaken the living or the dead!" She adds, "The man is a relative of ours, one of our nearest kin" (Ruth 2:20).

The bonding of these two women is growing stronger, as you can see in Naomi's use of "ours." She recognizes that her destiny and Ruth's are bound up together and gives us one more instance of the way the outsider, Ruth, is inexorably being drawn closer in to the band. Certainly no dummy, Naomi goes on to tell Ruth: "It is better, my daughter, that you go out with his young women, otherwise you might be bothered in another field" (Ruth 2:22). You can almost see the wheels starting to turn. Naomi, too, is aware of how attractive Ruth is, and that any healthy, right-minded young harvest worker would be bound to bother her—or at least try to get her attention. Why risk it, when the field-owner, the rich relative, is already taking an interest?

So Ruth sticks around in Boaz's field for both the barley and the wheat harvests, while Naomi does some long thinking about it all.

HARVEST—IN MORE WAYS THAN ONE

If Ruth has done her part by sparing Naomi the loss of face (and the hard labor) involved in gleaning, Naomi now prepares to do her part. She has come up with a plan to secure the future for both of them, and it centers on Boaz. The harvest is in, and the winnowing is being done, at the end of which there will be a terrific celebration. As a kid, I always imagined this would be like the Grape Harvest dance in the Hungarian community. You got to open the last year's vintage, and even normally sober adults were allowed to get downright effervescent. Naomi knows her harvests, and she unfolds her plan:

> *"Now wash and anoint yourself, and put on your best clothes and go down to the threshing floor; but do not make yourself known to the man until he has finished eating and drinking. When he lies down, observe the place where he lies; then, go and uncover his feet and lie down; and he will tell you what to do." (Ruth 3:3–4)*

And you thought Rebekah was a manipulator! Naomi is taking no chances about securing the future for herself and her daughter-in-law. She encourages Ruth to get all gussied up, put on her best dress, and sashay down to the harvest dance, where Boaz and the boys will be whooping it up. However, she doesn't have it in mind that Ruth will simply go as Boaz's date. Oh, no, she is much more explicit than that. Ruth is to wait until Boaz has had plenty to drink, and has finally conked out. Then she is to go and—good heavens!—uncover his feet.

The thing that your Sunday School teacher never told you (because probably your Sunday School teacher didn't know it) is that "uncovering his feet" was a euphemism for "uncovering his genitals." And no, that wasn't a big scene with Victorian artists, but possibly because they didn't know it was a euphemism, either.

At any rate, as we can see, Naomi is not pulling any punches here. In effect, Ruth is to wait until Boaz has passed out, and then go crawl into bed with him.

The next scene is actually quite delicious.

> *[Ruth] said to her, "All that you tell me I will do." So she went down to the threshing floor and did just as her mother-in-law had instructed her. When Boaz had eaten and drunk, and he was in a contented mood [i.e., feeling no pain], he went to lie down at the end of the heap of grain. Then she came stealthily and uncovered his feet,*

and lay down. At midnight the man was startled, and turned over,
and there, lying at his feet, was a woman! He said, "Who are you?"
And she answered, "I am Ruth, your servant; spread your cloak over
your servant, for you are next-of-kin." (Ruth 3:5–9)

You can almost picture the scene: Boaz, having had a bit too much, has finally fallen asleep. Midway in the night, he wakes up and ohmigod! here's a woman he has no recollection of having gone to bed with. If he's like most people in that situation, his first thought will be, "I must have been drunker than I thought," and his second is, "Oh, God! Who is it?"

Ruth gets right to the point. "I am Ruth, your servant; spread your cloak over your servant, for you are next-of-kin." I know, not exactly a romantic line. It's a reminder to Boaz that as the next-of-kin, he's the one who is supposed to marry the widow to raise up a son for his dead kinsman. (As a matter of fact, he is not even remotely obliged to marry Ruth, who is a foreigner and only Naomi's daughter-in-law. He would technically be obliged to marry Naomi. Everyone in the story knows this, but Naomi is certainly no dim bulb. She hasn't gussied herself up and gone to the harvest field. She knows her Law, but she knows her kinsman Boaz better.)

One way or another, Boaz realizes he's been had.

On the other hand, he doesn't seem to be too unhappy about the prospect. After all, it's Ruth.

He said, "May you be blessed by the LORD, my daughter; this last
instance of your loyalty is better than the first; you have not gone
after young men, whether poor or rich. And now, my daughter, do
not be afraid, I will do for you all that you ask, for all the assembly of
my people know that you are a worthy woman." (Ruth 3:10–11)

This is a truly odd little speech (especially under the circumstances), until we look at it closely. Boaz recognizes that, as a woman who's not really embedded in the family group, she could have sought a match on her own, independent of Naomi, with a younger man. She's instead offered to secure Naomi's future by invoking the Levirate law: in a sense, Ruth's first child will be regarded as Naomi's as much as her own, which wouldn't be true if she married outside the family. Boaz, too, recognizes this as true generosity of heart and is prepared to answer any objections in case the community raises the legal point of Ruth's being a foreigner: they all know she's worthy enough to be brought into the community.

To add a little twist of suspense, we now learn that Boaz is not, in fact, the closest near kin. There's another man even more closely related, and if that man chooses to marry Ruth, Boaz must defer to him (Ruth 3:12).

HEADING FOR A HAPPY ENDING

They spend the rest of the night together (no more details are provided by the text), and Boaz is anxious to get Ruth on her way back home before anyone else wakes up. (Complying with the Levirate law is one thing; but gossip is gossip, and this is a small town.) He sends her home with enough grain to keep her and Naomi going for weeks. Again, the woman who was sent home to Bethlehem emptied out by life is being filled (Ruth 3:12–17).

Naomi is practically rubbing her hands together in glee. "Wait, my daughter, until you learn how the matter turns out, for the man will not rest, but will settle the matter today" (Ruth 3:18).

The scene at the town gate (Ruth 4:1–10) has its own element of humor. Boaz goes to the town gate to set the marriage claim in motion. In the days before regular law courts and written contracts, transacting business "in the town gate" simply meant going into a public place where you could find the required number of witnesses to make a transaction legal and binding. Hence, Boaz immediately goes to the town gate, where he finds the closest kinsman of Naomi's, and ten elders (a *minyan*).

Shrewdly, he begins by telling the kinsman that Naomi wants to sell a field that was owned by their dead kinsman, Elimelech. Rather than let it be sold outside the family, the next of kin was expected, if possible, to redeem the land. To our dismay, the kinsman promptly and happily says he'll act as next-of-kin. Oops.

Boaz now springs his trap. "The day you acquire the field from the hand of Naomi, you are also acquiring Ruth the Moabite, the widow of the dead man, to maintain the dead man's name on his inheritance" (Ruth 4:5).

The kinsman promptly backs out: a son born to him and Ruth would be regarded as the son of her dead husband, and he can't marry her without damaging his own inheritance. He gives Boaz the right to act as next-of-kin, which Boaz promptly does. As long as he has the witnesses right there, he makes it official. He's acquired the field, and he's acquired Ruth.

> Then all the people who were at the gate, along with the elders, said,
> "We are witnesses. May the LORD make the woman who is coming
> into your house like Rachel and Leah, who together built up the
> house of Israel. May you produce children in Ephrathah and bestow a
> name in Bethlehem; and, through the children that the LORD will
> give you by this young woman, may your house be like the house of
> Perez, whom Tamar bore to Judah." (Ruth 4:11–12)

Already, Ruth is being woven into the fabric of the community, her name paired with the ancestral ones.

And Who Lived Happily Ever After?

Since this isn't a Harlequin Romance, but a Middle Eastern story, the "happily ever after" part of the story glides right past Ruth and Boaz, and the focus immediately shifts back to Naomi, where the story started.

Ruth and Boaz indeed marry and have a son, and the women in the community hasten to congratulate Naomi, telling her, "Blessed be the LORD, who has not left you this day without next-of-kin; and may his name be renowned in Israel! He shall be to you a restorer of life and a nourisher of your old age; for your daughter-in-law who loves you, who is more to you than seven sons, has borne him" (Ruth 4:14–15).

Even the community recognizes the depth of the bond that has kept these two women together.

> *Then Naomi took the child and laid him in her bosom, and became his nurse. The women of the neighborhood gave him a name, saying, "A son has been born to Naomi." They named him Obed; he became the father of Jesse, the father of David. (Ruth 4:16–17)*

Notice several things here. For the first time, we are really seeing a story that is set in the context of a community, not merely a family. All the earlier stories took place in the family, the clan. This one is dominated by family themes, but Naomi is a member of the community of Bethlehem, who goes out from it and returns to it. Her plight has been witnessed by the women who knew her before she left. The local workers at the harvest have observed the care her daughter-in-law has taken of her. The town elders have recognized the marriage of Ruth and Boaz not simply as a private marriage contract, but as an exercise of Levirate law to keep Elimelech's name alive in the community.

It's the women of the community who bless Naomi and recognize that God has restored her to the community. "A son has been born to Naomi," they say in recognition of her restoration. Moreover, they actually name the child.

We end with a short genealogy that reminds us that the newborn child can be traced back to Perez. Perez was the son of Judah and Tamar, and hence the grandson of Jacob. The child is a direct descendent of Abraham. But the real punch line of the story is that the child is the father of Jesse, who is the father of David.

Ruth, the Moabite, the foreigner, is the great-grandmother of Israel's greatest king. Not only has the community reached out and gathered her in, but her descendents will be knit into the Royal House. This was decidedly not lost on the story's hearers, not then or in subsequent generations.

Even in the Gospel of Matthew, in the genealogy of Jesus (Matthew 1:1–17), the writer gives a meticulous account tying Jesus to the line of

Abraham, and to the line of King David. As usual, it's largely a "So-and-So the Son of Such-and-Such" document, with a huge exception. There are four women listed in the genealogy, and every one of them is either a scandal or a foreigner, or both! They are Tamar, who gets pregnant by her father-in-law (Genesis 38), Rahab, the prostitute who shelters Joshua and his friends when they go to spy on Jericho (Joshua 2), Bathsheba, whose husband Uriah is killed by King David so he can marry her (2 Samuel 11–12), and Ruth herself.

Yes, the theme persists. God keeps bringing outsiders in, keeps taking strangers and creating a family out of them, as we see in the story of Ruth and Naomi.

True, God doesn't stand center stage in this one, as God stands in the story of Abraham and Isaac. God is quietly off stage, in the wings—or in the human heart—where God is usually found. God calls people through other people; God builds a family through people like Ruth and Naomi, who would find each other and hold fast in the tough times, support each other through the death of their hopes and through to the birth of a new future.

True, they may not always do it the way your Sunday School teachers wanted you to know they did. But they did it, with wit and humor and a knowledge that the real world is an earthy place, and the storytellers weren't embarrassed by the fact that King David's great-grandmother had what practically amounted to a shotgun wedding, biblical style.

God wouldn't be embarrassed, either. God is too busy rejoicing.

MARGARET'S STORY

I suppose you could call my story "Ruth and Naomi in Edinburgh." Only Ruth and Naomi were actually named Melissa and Alice, and it wasn't just two women trying to survive. It was two women and a baby girl. It's quite a story all the same.

Melissa was my grandmother, and she fell madly in love with a boy named Douglas and married him when she was barely out of her teens. In Scotland, you know, when you marry you're really marrying the whole family—the clan—and its tradition, and in this case it was the Army Tradition. Douglas' father was one of those spit-and-polish army sergeants who are the real salt of the earth and fiercely proud of their regiments. So when World War I started, there was no question of Douglas staying out. He wouldn't have wanted to.

Melissa's mother-in-law, Alice, had been an Army wife all her married life, and she didn't have much patience with Melissa's tears and anxieties. Things were not always easy between the two women. Alice was pretty peppery and her usual response to crises was, "God'll provide, but ye canna expect him to reach out and do the washin' oop for ye." I can just hear her, too, as it was something Melissa learned to say pretty firmly to her own children years later!

World War I was so unbelievably destructive. There were whole towns where there was barely a man between eighteen and forty left alive and whole afterwards. Douglas' father was killed during the first winter, and for all her self-control, Alice was devastated. Oddly enough, it brought the two women closer, because suddenly Melissa found that she could be the strong one, helping to keep life going for Alice.

Amazingly, Douglas survived till very near the end, though he was wounded several times. He actually got a leave not long before the war ended, and it was during that leave that Melissa became pregnant. But he never lived to see his child. Of all the bitter ironies, he was killed just two weeks before the Armistice was signed.

So there they were: two widows in a country crowded with widows, and a baby on the way.

Well, there was something in Alice's "God'll provide, but ye canna expect him to reach oot and do the washin' oop for ye" attitude that probably meant survival for both of them. Because, when you come down to it, all they had was each other. Alice decided that the only thing for it was to go where they had a chance of making a new life for themselves, which certainly wasn't the village where they were living. So the two of them picked up stakes and headed for Edinburgh, where Alice had a cousin who owned a fish and chips shop and was willing to give them some work. Besides that, Alice found work at what they called a French laundry in those days—a dry cleaning place, we'd call it.

Pretty soon my grandmother's daughter arrived on the scene, and there were two women and a baby, just about staying alive. But Alice was no fool. She noticed that a lot of men came into the shop to buy their lunch during the day, but in the evenings it was mostly women picking up something for their families' dinner. So she always saw to it that Melissa was the one handing out fish and chips at lunch time, while she took over in the evenings.

There were plenty of men who were only too happy to flirt with the pretty widow, or even invite her out, but Alice was the one who decided who was and wasn't acceptable, and when a young man named Jim who had his own insurance agency started coming in, she figured this was the one. The problem was how to fit Melissa out for a date. Everything they owned was dull, shabby, and darned in half a dozen places.

As far as Alice was concerned, that was no problem at all. Since God hadn't provided the wardrobe, God obviously expected Alice to reach out her own hand and do something. And reach out she did! Whenever Jim asked Melissa out, Alice simply went through the dry cleaning in the store where she worked, and whatever looked best or most glamorous simply went missing for a day or two. She wasn't stealing; she intended to take it back. And she didn't think God would mind if she just "borrowed" it for an evening. Sometimes the two women had to more or less sew the dress on Melissa to take in the slack, and once they had to drape silk shawls all over her to conceal the fact that the bodice was too tight to button in back, but off Melissa would go, dressed to the nines, and with luck the dress would be back on the rack before its owner came to call for it.

Fortunately Alice never got caught smuggling a customer's dress out of the shop, and her little deception worked. Jim (who eventually became my grandfather, by the way), thought Melissa was simply the most attractive, best-dressed woman he'd ever seen, and before long he proposed to her. Needless to say, he was taking on Alice as well as Melissa and the baby, because the two women were closer than any mother and daughter could be by that time. They had seen each other through the worst, God had provided after a fashion, and Alice hadn't been afraid to reach out when God's provisions fell a little short.

I do have to add that Melissa always claimed that when she and Jim got married, Alice attended the wedding in a gown especially "borrowed" for the occasion, but it was positively the last time she ever reached out and borrowed anything.

QUESTIONS FOR STUDY AND REFLECTION

In reading the story:

- What does the narrative tell us about Ruth and Naomi's personalities?
- What does their relationship tell us?
- What might be called unusual about them?
- What strengths do each of them have?
- How do they use their strengths for each other's benefit?
- Where are they by the end of the story?

Self-reflection and learning:

- Do I have a Ruth or Naomi in my life?
- Where in my life am I like Naomi? Ruth?
- How do my own strengths and weaknesses work together?
- What light does this throw on my own story?

What questions and problems does this still leave unanswered or "in process"?

CHAPTER SEVEN

Judith: The Woman and the Warrior

THE PROBLEM OF JUDITH

First of all, let me admit that I like Judith. I always have. I liked her from the first time I saw one of those wonderful Renaissance portraits of Judith with the head of Holofernes when I was about eight. Artists have always adored Judith, too, apparently, since there are a surprising number of paintings showing Judith with the head of Holofernes. It offers such possibilities to artists who are big on anatomical verisimilitude. Think about it. It's a dynamite opportunity no artist can resist: all that gore and anatomical detail in the sprawling body and the decapitated head, plus a luscious-looking woman in filmy clothes. Wealthy buyers have always snapped up these paintings as soon as they were dry on the easel. It's sometimes hard to tell the difference between paintings of Judith with the head of Holofernes and Salome with the head of John the Baptist, a subject nearly as popular. I've always suspected that some artists just whipped up a basic scantily-clad-woman-with-decapitated-head and let the buyer decide who it was. There is, however, an infallible way of telling them apart. Salome's trophy head is tidily presented on a platter, and Judith is holding a sword. (I had no interest in pictures of Salome with John the Baptist as a kid: all she did was dance, while somebody else got the fun of cutting John's head off. But Judith, now—she really *did* it!)

Judith, now, indeed. She really did do it. Which, in some ways, constitutes the problem of Judith. Her story is so atypical of most women's stories that she's hard for most of us to identify with at first glance. We can relate to a Sarah, impatiently trying to nudge God along, or to a Leah, never feeling quite good enough in comparison to someone else. Many of us can easily identify with women who only survive with a little help from their friends, like Ruth and Naomi.

But Judith is something else. She's a woman, true, but she's also, in very explicit terms, a warrior, a woman who takes a sword and severs another warrior's head and delivers a city and a nation—and that's far outside the experience of any woman I've ever met. Come to think of it, it's outside the experience of any man I've met, too.

But there's a perennial fascination in Judith, not just for the artists, but for anyone who reads the story. It's a story in the grand old biblical mode, studded with grand old biblical themes—even though it's not an official part of the Old Testament. It is one of the apocryphal or deuterocanonical books, books that were written in the period between the last of the Old Testament books and before the writing of the New Testament, in that period that we loosely call "Hellenistic."

Most of these books were written in Greek, since Hebrew was no longer an everyday spoken language, and few practicing Jews could actually read it. In the Holy Land, Aramaic was already the common spoken language, but far more Jews lived outside the Holy Land than in it. They lived all over the civilized world, where Greek was the universal language. In fact, they read the Scriptures in Greek translation.

Judith, then, was one of the Greek works that became enormously important to Jews of the Diaspora, scattered through the Hellenistic world, books that had specifically Jewish themes either spiritually or historically (1 and 2 Maccabees, for instance), and often purported to be set in ancient times. They were popular religious works that probably had a great emotional impact on their readers for a variety of reasons, but they were never actually accepted in the canon of the Scripture.

But some of these books gripped both hearts and imaginations, and became part of the cultural, if not the religious fabric of the late Hellenistic Jewish world, and later the early Christian one. Judith, along with other late Hellenistic works which weren't included in either the Old or the New Testaments, was included as part of the Apocrypha, where she remained. The Protestant Reformers, however, generally excluded the Apocrypha from their Bibles, sticking to the Old and New Testaments, while the Catholic Church continued to include it. For this reason, many of us who were raised in Protestant traditions don't know Judith at all and won't find her in the Bibles on our shelves.

You may, in fact, have to go out and buy a translation of the Bible that includes the Apocrypha, or get onto the Internet to download the book. Do it. You'll find Judith well worth getting acquainted with. Her story may not be typical, but she still has much to teach us.

CHALLENGING THE ASSUMPTIONS

First of all, let me say up front that some of the reasons why the Reformers weren't comfortable with Judith are still true today. This is at best a morally ambiguous story centered on a woman who challenges the assumptions almost all Westerners have made about women for centuries—especially assumptions about *religious* women. Judith is a pious woman whose life centers around fasting and prayer, but during the course of the story she lies (or at least equivocates pretty strenuously), she deliberately plays the seductress, and she finally murders in cold blood a man who is sound asleep and cannot defend himself. Her actions are positively grisly, and they're applauded as having their source and focus in God.

She's also a woman of almost staggering courage, who places herself in the most dangerous of positions, with no safeguards, and undertakes a task knowing that, if she fails, both she and her people will surely die. She does it for no other reason than that she knows it must be done to preserve God's people.

She's a woman whose personality shines through the story so clearly that, even when we understand the ambiguities, we find ourselves setting them aside and abandoning ourselves to the tension, the ironic humor, the surprise, and the triumph of the story. Judith is cut in a heroic mold that's right up there with young David and the fighters of the Warsaw Ghetto.

Judith is, however, a work of fiction, a well-crafted little novella written by an obviously skilled storyteller, rather than a simple retelling of a story that was passed down through the generations. Keep in mind, however, that "factual" and "true" don't necessarily mean the same thing. This isn't a factual story, but any writer or reader alive knows that fiction is sometimes the most powerful way of conveying certain truths, and Judith rings true even on the biblical scale. It's a story of the reversals God specializes in, and the writer sets the stage carefully. The strong will be balanced against the weak, the powerful against the powerless, the ferocious warrior against the seemingly frail widow.

SETTING THE STAGE

A full half of the story takes place before Judith even enters the scene (she doesn't appear until Chapter 8 of a sixteen-chapter book), so take heart. There's less here to read than you think.

I remember a popular poster from the '60s: "Suppose they gave a war and nobody came?" That's how Judith opens. Nebuchadnezzar, King of the Assyrians, whose Empire has conquered most of the known world, wants to go to war against Arphaxad, King of the Medes. He calls on all the surrounding nations who owe him military support to send troops to fight for him. Nobody comes, so he has to wage the war all by himself. He's furious that nobody will come to his aid, and Nebuchadnezzar in a rage is fairly awesome to behold. He swears ". . . that he would take revenge on the whole territory of Cilicia and Damascus and Syria, that he would kill with his sword also all the inhabitants of the land of Moab, and the people of Ammon, and all Judea, and everyone in Egypt, as far as the coasts of the two seas" (Judith 1:12).

Once he has defeated Arphaxad, he's ready for his revenge, and summons his chief general, Holofernes.

"Thus says the Great King, the lord of the whole earth: . . . [I] will cover the whole face of the earth with the feet of my troops, to whom I will hand them over to be plundered. Their wounded shall fill their ravines and gullies, and the swelling river shall be filled with their dead. . . . [T]o those who resist show no mercy, but hand them over to slaughter and plunder throughout your whole region. For as I live, and by the power of my kingdom, what I have spoken I will accomplish by my own hand." (Judith 2:5–12)

The last sentence is one of the earliest bits of irony in the book. Nebuchadnezzar is speaking figuratively, since he himself won't lift a finger—he turns the job over to his troops. Judith, on the other hand, really will accomplish what she promises with her own hand.

Holofernes, a true super-achiever, promptly sets out to do the king's bidding, and for several chapters we're given a brisk account of slaughtering, burning, pillaging, and general mayhem, in which Holofernes proves how literally he takes his king's commandments. We can spare ourselves most of this, except for one interesting passage. The people of the seacoast, trying to placate the king's fury, send gracious messages of surrender. Holofernes, however, isn't impressed.

These people and all in the countryside welcomed him with garlands and dances and tambourines. Yet he demolished all their shrines and cut down their sacred groves; for he had been commissioned to destroy all the gods of the land, so that all nations should worship Nebuchadnezzar alone, and that all their dialects and tribes should call upon him as a god. (Judith 3:7–8)

This not only gives us a measure of Holofernes, but sets one of the themes involved in the book. The Assyrian ruler wants to be worshiped as a god; the Jews have only one God. The contest is now shifted to a new ground. It's not simply a war between the Assyrian empire and its disobedient political vassals: it's about obedience in a deeper sense.

The Jews, having just returned from exile in Bablyon, hear this story with horror and determine to resist rather than surrender. They don sackcloth, fast, and pray, even draping the altar of the temple with sackcloth,

Praying fervently to the God of Israel not to allow their infants to be carried off and their wives to be taken as booty, and the towns they had inherited to be destroyed, and the sanctuary to be profaned and

desecrated to the malicious joy of the Gentiles. The Lord heard their
prayers and had regard for their distress; for the people fasted for
many days throughout Judea and in Jerusalem before the sanctuary
of the Lord Almighty. (Judith 4:12–13)

Not only do they prepare themselves spiritually, but they instantly move to capture the passes and the hill-forts that Holofernes will have to pass to reach Jerusalem.

Astonished that anyone will resist him, Holofernes demands to know who these "hill-people" are. Achior, King of the Ammonites, recites a mini-history of the Jews, in astonishing detail, starting with their leaving Ur and wandering in Canaan, their sojourn in Egypt and the Exodus, the conquest of Canaan and their subsequent history. He then comes to the point:

As long as they did not sin against their God they prospered, for the
God who hates iniquity is with them. But when they departed from
the way he had prescribed for them, they were utterly defeated in
many battles and were led away captive to a foreign land. The temple
of their God was razed to the ground, and their towns were occupied
by their enemies. (Judith 5:17–18)

Only if they have abandoned God can they be defeated, Achior tells him; otherwise "their Lord and God will defend them, and we shall become the laughingstock of the whole world" (Judith 5:21).

Furious at the thought that Achior doubts their ability to conquer these mere hill-people, the Assyrians threaten Achior with death, but eventually decide simply to send him to the Israelites, to be destroyed along with them. They bind him and abandon him outside the town of Bethulia, the first town they intend to destroy. (Again, the author is setting up an ironical point: Achior will survive precisely because he is abandoned outside Bethulia.)

Holofernes moves to capture the springs from which the town of Bethulia draws its water, the siege begins, and both the noose around the town, and the plot, tighten. The people of Bethulia hold out as long as their water does and then decide it's better to surrender to Holofernes than to watch their children die. Their magistrates, Uzziah, Chabris, and Charmis, are no warriors. Uzziah can only temporize. Wait five days, he says; if God doesn't save us by then, we can surrender.

If this were a TV mini-series, the music would rise and swell dramatically, and there'd be a commercial, with a trailer showing you some exciting scenes from tomorrow's episode (no doubt featuring shots of Judith in her seductive finery).

ENTER JUDITH

Indeed, right on cue, Judith enters the story (Judith 8:1–9). She's introduced via a genealogy that traces her back to Israel (Jacob) himself, and as the widow of Manasseh "who belonged to her tribe and family." This is a surprising reversal of the usual reference; it's usually the woman who's described as coming from her husband's family and tribe. Some scholars suggest that this indicates that Judith may have been the heiress of a wealthy man who had no sons. On his death, she'd have been married to one of her kin, in much the same way Boaz marries Ruth, to keep her property in the family. As we'll see in her subsequent behavior, she does act more like a woman used to handling wealth and power than she does like an ordinary modest widow.

> Judith remained as a widow for three years and four months at home
> where she set up a tent for herself on the roof of her house. She put
> sackcloth around her waist and dressed in widow's clothing. She
> fasted all the days of her widowhood, except the day before the
> sabbath and the sabbath itself, the day before the new moon and the
> day of the new moon, and the festivals and days of rejoicing of the
> house of Israel. (Judith 8:4–6)

Judith, in other words, refused to live in the comfort of her no doubt luxurious home, but instead set up a more primitive place for herself on the roof. She dressed in poor clothing and fasted on every day except the ones when fasting was specifically forbidden. Moreover, we're told, she was beautiful, and her husband Manasseh had left her considerable wealth, which she maintained. As a final note, the narrator adds, "No one spoke ill of her, for she feared God with great devotion" (Judith 8:8).

This in itself says something. Few women with Judith's advantages, in terms of wealth and looks, could escape being objects of envy and criticism.

Judith is an altogether unusual character, even in this brief glimpse. She's remained a widow for over three years without re-marrying, a thing almost unheard of in this society, and she herself maintains her late husband's estate (which may originally have been hers).

A fairly astonishing woman. The next passage is even more astonishing. When she hears what the people of Bethulia are saying, and what Uzziah has said to them, "she sent her maid, *who was in charge of all she possessed,* to summon Uzziah and Chabris and Charmis, the elders of her town. They came to her" (Judith 8:10–11).

First, she has a woman in charge of her property, not a man. As the owner and administrator of her estate, she of course has the right to put whomever she likes in charge. Judith has chosen a woman.[12] This, too, says something about her sense of authority. She isn't meant to be seen as a woman who relies on a man to care for her affairs: she herself directs the maid, who is actually a slave.

Next, she not only summons the elders, but they immediately respond by coming to her. This is real social clout, even for an Israelite man to exercise, much less a woman.

Oh, but it gets more intriguing yet. Not only does she summon the elders, but she proceeds to lecture them!

> *"Who are you to put God to the test today, and to set yourselves up in the place of God in human affairs? You are putting the Lord Almighty to the test, but you will never learn anything! You cannot plumb the depths of the human heart or understand the workings of the human mind; how do you expect to search out God, who made all these things, and find out his mind or comprehend his thought?"*
> *(Judith 8:12–14)*

In fact, she gives them a brisk little lecture in contemporary theology, explaining that Israel was defeated in the past when it worshiped false gods, but their present steadfastness should encourage them (Judith 8:18–20). She's too cautious to promise that God will deliver them, but she notes that even if they're defeated, their steadfastness still matters. Surely God will repay the violation of his sanctuary, and their very captivity will bring disgrace on the Gentiles' heads.

She ends with a rousing speech:

> *"Therefore, my brothers, let us set an example to our kindred, for their lives depend upon us, and the sanctuary—both the temple and the altar—rests upon us. In spite of everything let us give thanks to the Lord our God, who is putting us to the test as he did our ancestors. Remember what he did with Abraham, and how he tested Isaac, and what happened to Jacob in Syrian Mesopotamia, while he was tending the sheep of Laban, his mother's brother. For he has not tried us with fire, as he did them, to search their hearts, nor has he taken vengeance on us; but the Lord scourges those who are close to him in order to admonish them." (Judith 8:24–27)*

Properly chastened—or braced—Uzziah thanks her and asks Judith to pray that God will send rain to fill their cisterns.

But Judith has no use for Uzziah's plan: she has one of her own, and she doesn't need to consult anyone about how to put it into effect.

> *"Listen to me. I am about to do something that will go down through all generations of our descendants. Stand at the town gate tonight so*

> *that I may go out with my maid; and within the days after which*
> *you have promised to surrender the town to our enemies, the Lord*
> *will deliver Israel by my hand. Only, do not try to find out what I am*
> *doing; for I will not tell you until I have finished what I am about*
> *to do." (Judith 8:32–34)*

Notice that Judith, like Nebuchadnezzar, promises to achieve something by her own hand. But Judith, unlike the Great King, means it, as we shall see. Moreover, she wants to play this close to her chest. She won't tell anyone what she intends. This perhaps isn't so surprising. What *is* surprising is how meekly the three agree to her orders. Yes, you'll notice that she doesn't ask them to do anything: she tells them. This is definitely not your usual Jewish widow of that time.

THE WIDOW MAKES READY

Judith (who has probably arrayed herself in suitably impressive attire to entertain the elders), now takes off her finery and uncovers her sackcloth, puts ashes on her head, and prostrates herself. She times this so that she begins her prayer exactly when the evening incense is being offered in the temple in Jerusalem. Judith, after all, isn't praying for herself, but on behalf of the whole people of Israel. Her prayer is meant to be seen as part of the prayer being offered by the priests at that very moment (Judith 9:1).

She begins with a surprisingly fierce passage:

> *"O Lord God of my ancestor Simeon, to whom you gave a sword to*
> *take revenge on those strangers who had torn off a virgin's clothing to*
> *defile her, and exposed her thighs to put her to shame, and polluted*
> *her womb to disgrace her; for you said, 'It shall not be done'—yet*
> *they did it." (Judith 9:2)*

Evocative words indeed! Judith is referring to Genesis 34, in which Simeon and Levi, Jacob's son, slaughter all the men of Hamor and Shechem to avenge the rape of their sister Dinah. They not only kill all the men, but destroy the town and carry away all its goods, animals, women, and children as plunder. She's invoking the spirit of one of the most violent episodes in her ancestral history. But oddly enough, she ends the bloody passage with, "O God, my God, hear me also, a widow" (Judith 9:4).

It's not really a change of subject, for Judith's widowhood will be essential to what follows:

> *"Look at their pride, and send your wrath upon their heads. Give to*
> *me, a widow, the strong hand to do what I plan. By the deceit of my*
> *lips strike down the slave with the prince and the prince with his*

servant; crush their arrogance by the hand of a woman."
(Judith 9:9–10)

She's not simply asking God to crush the enemy, but to crush the enemy in a way that adds unbearable disgrace to his defeat. Not only will his power be humbled, but the power of the world's greatest military machine will be humbled by a mere widow. "For your strength does not depend on numbers, nor your might on the powerful. But you are the God of the lowly, helper of the oppressed, upholder of the weak, protector of the forsaken, savior of those without hope" (Judith 9:11).

She ends with a reminder that only God is god, as if in counterpoint to Holofernes' arrogant claim that everyone will worship Nebuchadnezzar alone (Judith 9:14).

The Warrior Arms Herself

Judith now finishes her prayer and goes into the luxurious house, calling for her maid. She has prepared herself spiritually; now she will complete the process. Judith the warrior arms herself for battle.

> *She removed the sackcloth she had been wearing, took off her widow's garments, bathed her body with water, and anointed herself with precious ointment. [Unlike the thirsty townsfolk, who must draw from the drying public wells, Judith as a wealthy woman would have had her own cistern, possibly even a pool.] She combed her hair, put on a tiara, and dressed herself in the festive attire that she used to wear while her husband Manasseh was living. She put sandals on her feet, and put on her anklets, bracelets, rings, earrings, and all her other jewelry. Thus she made herself very beautiful, to entice the eyes of all the men who might see her. (Judith 10:3–4)*

The reader, too, understands the irony of the passage. It sounds as if Judith is a woman getting ready for a feast, pampering herself with perfume and water, loading herself down with every piece of jewelry she has, arraying herself to "entice the eyes" of anyone who sees her. We're to understand that the jewels, the rings, the sandals, the perfume—what most would have considered frivolous things—will be used to destroy the Assyrians.

Arming herself in another way, she takes food that's ritually clean, and the dishes for preparing it, and places them in a bag she hands to her maid (Judith 10:5). She'll be doing battle for God, and as the reader has already been reminded several times in the story, those who break God's laws can be defeated by their enemies. Judith won't break even the smallest of God's laws to defeat Holofernes. She goes boldly to the gates and orders that they be opened to let her out, like a general ordering subordinates, and they obey her.

When they had done this, Judith went out, accompanied by her
maid. The men of the town watched her until she had gone down the
mountain and passed through the valley, where they lost sight of her.
(Judith 10:10)

The writer gives us a nice dramatic moment here, leaving the reader standing on the walls, watching the two women diminish slowly in the distance, small figures who are, in effect, proposing to do battle with the entire Assyrian War Machine.

The narration picks up quite briskly with Judith's arrival in the valley. This is truly an excellent writer, who suddenly shifts us to the Assyrian patrol who accost the two women, demanding to know who they are. Judith doesn't hesitate for a fraction of a second to lie about it:

"I am a daughter of the Hebrews, but I am fleeing from them, for
they are about to be handed over to you to be devoured. I am on my
way to see Holofernes the commander of your army, to give him a
true report; I will show him a way by which he can go and capture all
the hill country without losing one of his men, captured or slain."
(Judith 10:12–13)

The soldiers react very much as you would expect: they are bowled over by Judith's beauty, as much as by her message. There is real humor in what follows: "Go at once to his tent; some of us will escort you and hand you over to him. . . . They chose from their number a hundred men to accompany her and her maid, and they brought them to the tent of Holofernes" (Judith 10:15–17). In other words, every man in the valley must have volunteered to escort Judith and her maid to the camp.

Moreover, the soldiers in camp are similarly smitten by Judith. The entire camp gathers around to see her. No doubt thinking of the women who will be their booty when Bethulia falls, they say: "It is not wise to leave one of their men alive, for if we let them go they will be able to beguile the whole world!" (Judith 10:19).

When Judith's arrival is announced, "Holofernes was resting on his bed under a canopy that was woven with purple and gold, emeralds and other precious stones" (Judith 10:21). Unheard of luxury for a military commander on campaign, but the canopy will become significant later.

Holofernes greets her with reassurance—which, ironically, Judith doesn't need. She in turn speaks in the first of some wonderful cross-talk passages: "I will say nothing false to my lord this night. If you follow out the words of your servant, God will accomplish something through you, and my lord will not fail to achieve his purposes" (Judith 11:5–6). What Judith means, and what Holofernes thinks she means, are two different things.

Judith now unfolds the first part of her plan: she is buying time for Bethulia. She reminds him of what Achior has told him:

> *Therefore, lord and master, do not disregard what he said, but keep it in your mind, for it is true. Indeed our nation cannot be punished, nor can the sword prevail against them, unless they sin against their God.* (Judith 11:10)

She weaves an elaborate falsehood, telling Holofernes that the people of Bethulia, whose food is running out, propose to defy God's laws by eating the first-fruits that have been consecrated to God for the priests, and have sent to Jerusalem for confirmation that they may do this. As soon as confirmation comes back, and the people of Bethulia eat, Holofernes will be able to go in and slay them all. Meanwhile she'll go out and pray every night, until God gives her the sign that Holofernes can strike (Judith 11:12–18).

At the very end of this, she adds: "Then I will lead you through Judea, until you come to Jerusalem; there I will set your throne" (Judith 11:19).

Pleased, Holofernes invites Judith to dine with him, but she excuses herself, since she can only eat her own, ritually clean, food. Holofernes asks if he can find more of her food if she runs out, and Judith's answer positively gives us a little frisson of delicious horror: "As surely as you live, my lord, your servant will not use up the supplies I have with me before the Lord carries out by my hand what he has determined" (Judith 12:4).

JUDITH SPRINGS THE TRAP

For three days, Judith lulls the Assyrians by following an unvarying routine. Each night she goes out to the valley and ritually bathes in a spring, returns to her tent, fasts and prays all day, and eats when the evening comes. On the fourth day, Holofernes, still tantalized by the beautiful widow, tells his servant Bagoas, "Go and persuade the Hebrew woman who is in your care to join us and to eat and drink with us. For it would be a disgrace if we let such a woman go without having intercourse with her. If we do not seduce her, she will laugh at us" (Judith 12:11–12).

No reader, by now, would be surprised: it simply means that Judith's strategy is working. Bagoas, the eunuch, comes and delivers a rather oily little speech, addressing Judith as "this pretty girl," which only shows us how thoroughly Judith has hoodwinked the Assyrians. She smiles sweetly and replies, "Who am I to refuse my lord? Whatever pleases him I will do at once, and it will be a joy to me until the day of my death" (Judith 12:14).

She prepares for battle, putting on her finery and having her maid unroll a lambskin for her to recline on at Holofernes' feet. It doesn't take a great imagination to see Holofernes positively salivating as Judith stretches out on the lambskin. He invites her to drink. Again, her reply is prime. "I will gladly drink, my lord, because today is the greatest day in my whole life" (Judith 12:18). Ah! Be still my heart! must be Holofernes response.

Meanwhile, he starts drinking—more, in fact, than he has ever drunk in his life, until even the servants give up and turn in, leaving Holofernes and the widow all alone in the tent. Holofernes falls into a drunken sleep. In a scene worthy of something out of an Elizabethan drama, Judith stands at the bedside and prays: "O Lord God of all might, look in this hour on the work of my hands for the exaltation of Jerusalem. Now indeed is the time to help your heritage and to carry out my design to destroy the enemies who have risen up against us" (Judith 13:4–5).

Without any further delay, she takes Holofernes' own sword, seizes him by the hair and cuts his head off with two powerful strokes, wraps the head in the canopy of his bed (that luxurious canopy!) and calmly goes out and hands it to the maid to put in the food bag.

The two of them proceed with their evening routine, going out to the springs in the valley as if to bathe, but instead going directly on to Bethulia. Any elaboration of the scene would be anticlimax.

She and the maid return to Bethulia, where she praises God for destroying Israel's enemies by her hand, and at the climax of her speech "she pulled the head out of the bag and showed it to them, and said, 'See here, the head of Holofernes, the commander of the Assyrian army, and here is the canopy beneath which he lay in his drunken stupor. The Lord has struck him down by the hand of a woman'" (Judith 13:15).

The enemy is not only slain, but disgraced forever.

Judith the Commander

Almost at once, Judith the warrior, victorious from her own battle, becomes Judith the commander, telling the men of Bethulia to arm and go out as if they were going to attack, but to wait. The Assyrians, she knows, will rush to tell Holofernes and discover his headless body. The Israelites can then attack the panic-stricken Assyrians and destroy them (Judith 14:1–5).

The Israelites are overjoyed. Even Achior, listening to Judith's story, is so overwhelmed by God's mighty deliverance through a woman's hands that he immediately converts (Judith 14:10).

Judith's plan is carried out at once. When Bagoas, the King's eunuch, goes to the tent and discovers the body, he is well-repaid for having treated Judith so patronizingly. He cries: "The slaves have tricked us! One Hebrew woman has brought disgrace on the house of King Nebuchadnezzar. Look, Holofernes is lying on the ground, and his head is missing!" (Judith 14:18).

Not only do the men of Bethulia rout the Assyrians, but of course the other towns rise against them, as well, and the defeat of the Assyrians is calamitously complete. Even the elders in Jerusalem come out to see the astonishing deliverance that the widow has handed them. When the Assyrian camp is plundered, they award Judith Holofernes' tent and goods, not to mention his canopy.

> *All the women of Israel gathered to see her, and blessed her, and some*
> *of them performed a dance in her honor. She took ivy-wreathed*
> *wands in her hands and distributed them to the women who were*
> *with her; and she and those who were with her crowned themselves*
> *with olive wreaths. She went before all the people in the dance,*
> *leading all the women, while all the men of Israel followed, bearing*
> *their arms and wearing garlands and singing hymns.*
> *(Judith 15:12–13)*

All right, it's a decidedly Hellenistic way of celebrating, especially the ivy-wreathed wands and the crowning with olive wreaths, but the writer was a Hellenized Jew who wanted his readers to see this as a true victory celebration, with all the trappings usually associated with official triumphs. Judith has contended as a warrior: she will be feted as one, is the implication.

The ending passage of the triumph, the glorious Hymn of Judith, could be straight out of the older Scriptures. It is reminiscent of Miriam's exultant hymn on the shores of the Red Sea, when the Egyptians have been drowned. Parts of it could be straight out of the Psalms. The writer knows his Scriptures and sounds all the fervent and triumphant notes.

Judith herself, at one point, sings:

> *"He boasted that he would burn up my territory,*
> *and kill my young men with the sword,*
> *and dash my infants to the ground,*
> *and seize my children as booty,*
> *and take my virgins as spoil.*
> *But the Lord Almighty has foiled them*
> *by the hand of a woman." (Judith 16:4–5)*

Judith, in other words, is actually speaking as Israel itself, rather than as a single person. She has embodied her people and acted on their behalf, God's instrument. Ironically, she continues:

> *"Her sandal ravished his eyes,*
> *her beauty captivated his mind,*
> *and the sword severed his neck!*
> *The Persians trembled at her boldness,*
> *the Medes were daunted at her daring.*
> *Then my oppressed people shouted;*
> *my weak people cried out, and the enemy trembled;*

they lifted up their voices,
and the enemy were turned back.
Sons of slave-girls pierced them through
and wounded them like the children of fugitives;
they perished before the army of my Lord."
(Judith 16:9–12)

The reversal is complete: the slaves, the weak, the oppressed have risen and the Lord has given them victory. The theme sounded at the beginning is complete. In one final irony, Judith dedicates the canopy of Holofernes' bed as a votive offering in the temple.

Judith at Rest

At the end, she returns to her own home, to resume the quiet life she had abandoned to save Israel. "Many desired to marry her, but she gave herself to no man all the days of her life after her husband Manasseh died and was gathered to his people" (Judith 16:22).

Judith remains her own woman, freeing the maid who shared her danger (though we're never to know the woman's name). But something interesting happens in this little coda that we have to notice. She married no one in "all the days of her life after her husband Manasseh died." Suddenly, after eight chapters of acting with an awesome independence, Judith is again the widow of Manasseh. "She died in Bethulia, and they buried her in the cave of her husband Manasseh; and the house of Israel mourned her for seven days. Before she died she distributed her property to all those who were next of kin to her husband Manasseh, and to her own nearest kindred" (Judith 16:23–24).

So much for Judith the Warrior. It's been suggested that it was a later editor who added all those little references to "Manasseh her husband," and in fact it makes sense. The storyteller has set before us an awesomely courageous woman, who acts with duplicity and daring when her countrymen merely dither about their fates. It's hard to imagine the writer ill at ease with the Judith who's held up as a vision of both beauty and deadliness. But clearly, later generations weren't nearly so comfortable with this vision. It might, of course, give anyone's daughter ideas!

The conventional happy ending, too, seems tacked-on: "No one ever again spread terror among the Israelites during the lifetime of Judith, or for a long time after her death" (Judith 16:25). And they all lived happily ever after.

No, Judith the Warrior deserves a better ending than that, so let us turn to the last words in her song, the last words we hear from Judith herself:

"Woe to the nations that rise up against my people!
The Lord Almighty will take vengeance on them

in the day of judgment;
he will send fire and worms into their flesh;
they shall weep in pain for ever." (Judith 16:17)

Now, *that* sounds like Judith!

JEANNIE'S STORY

Judith wasn't one of the women I learned about as a little girl,
believe me. Sister Gemma and Sister Mary Sebastian and the other
nuns taught us about much nicer women. Like the Blessed Virgin
Mary, who certainly never would have put on perfume and powder to
go and call on some man. Or St. Therese, who looked too fragile even
to lift a sword, much less cut off somebody's head with it.

I got mixed messages about women. There were the holy women
I heard about in Catholic school, who were patient and pious and
ladylike. And then there were the real women I heard about from my
mother, who were brave and defiant and angry. I always thought
I should want to be like St. Anne or St. Agnes, especially because the
sisters tended to reward the girls who were like them. But, deplorably,
I really wanted to be like my mother and her friends, and I was afraid
the nuns wouldn't have liked that at all.

My mother grew up in a market town about ninety miles from
Paris. Her family were solid, middle class people who owned a small
restaurant, one of those places you see all over France, where everybody
in the family is kept busy, from Grandmère cooking in the kitchen
down to the children waiting on tables and washing up in the back. My
mother always worked there after school and in the evenings.

When the Germans occupied France, nothing much really
changed for a lot of people: they went on with their daily jobs, at least
on the surface. But even an agreeable-looking family who graciously
ushered German soldiers to their tables had their ways of fighting back.
Their restaurant was very popular with the soldiers, because the food
was tasty and inexpensive—and because my mother and her cousin
were young and pretty and waited on the tables. Little did they know
that when Grandmère prepared a plate of soup for a German soldier,
she spit in it before she put it on the tray. Then my mother or her cousin
would serve it to the German soldier with an especially charming smile.
One of my mother's favorite tricks was to let the dog lick the delicious
looking sausage before putting it on the plate. You wouldn't believe
some of the things they did to those plates before their unsuspecting
German customers sat down to eat, and I'm pretty sure my mother
never told me more than half of it.

You see? St. Anne would never have done that! But my mother did that, and a lot more besides. She was only fourteen when the Germans came, and she was this wholesome-looking schoolgirl who went to Mass every morning, came in to work at the restaurant as soon as school was over, and—this is the part that is incredible—was carrying information for the Resistance on practically a daily basis.

It was one advantage of being there in the restaurant, waiting on the German soldiers. Oh, yes, she could have taught Judith a thing or two. She would put on a pretty blouse, tuck a flower in her hair, and flirt like crazy with those German boys. And that's what most of them were, just young boys barely out of school, trying to impress a pretty girl with how important they were. She wasn't the only schoolgirl of fourteen or fifteen or sixteen who learned plenty of things while carrying on a flirtation over the soup plates, or in the bakery, or the inn where the soldiers went to have a glass of wine. They had a regular chain for passing the little items they learned on to the men in the local Resistance, sometimes carrying things in their school satchels when they went to Mass in the morning, and tucking the paper inside the missal in a particular pew. It sounds so simple, but two of her brothers' friends, boys no more than thirteen, were shot by the Germans because they were caught doing this.

Once, when her brother was supposed to deliver a packet of papers to someone, and he had sprained his ankle and couldn't go, my mother grabbed her girlfriend, took the papers, and off they went, as if they were taking a stroll just to flirt with the soldiers. Her friend deliberately broke the strap on her sandal, and while she was giggling and three German soldiers were laughing and trying to fix it for her, my mother was able to run around the side of the building and push the papers through a slot in the shutter. Fourteen years old, and they would have shot her if they knew what she was up to!

Did she think less of herself because she used what we'd call feminine wiles to trick the Germans? Don't be silly! The Germans kept a close eye on the strong young men, but nobody paid attention to a pretty, petite schoolgirl. She was a fourteen-year-old girl, not a forty-year-old man. She used what she had. She couldn't fly a plane or blow up a bridge. She didn't have a short-wave radio or a machine gun. She had hair that curled and a laugh that made men smile. She put flowers in her hair and joked and giggled and German soldiers died because of what she passed on. And French patriots lived. She knew that courage wasn't a thing of the body, but of the spirit.

Was she a hero? Oh, yes, she was that. She fought with the weapons that she had. But a saint? No. She wasn't anybody's saint, at least not the way the sisters defined it. Unless you count that other French saint, Joan of Arc. But I can see my mother as a Judith, maybe a little younger and a little less glamorous, but somebody who wasn't afraid to fight for what mattered to her.

My mother lived her whole life with that same kind of courage, just doing whatever had to be done as an ordinary woman, a wife and mother. She was also a religious woman. She went to Mass most days. She sent me to school with the nuns. She wanted me to be a good Catholic girl. But you know, I'm not sure it worked. What she was taught me more than what the nuns said about how you live your life. Though when I look back on it now, I suspect that some of those nuns admired my mother a lot more than they ever let on.

QUESTIONS FOR STUDY AND REFLECTION

In reading the story:

- What does the narrative tell us about Judith's social position?
- What do we learn about her picture of God?
- What kind of courage does she exhibit? What kind of craftiness?
- What do you think of the honors paid her?

Self-reflection and learning:

- Does Judith teach me something about how one wins?
- Have I ever done things "Judith's way"?
- Is she a person I could emulate?
- What parts of Judith do I want to own? Disown?

What questions and problems does this still leave unanswered or "in process"?

CHAPTER EIGHT

Esther: Genocide, Faith, and the Whole Megillah

THE JOY—AND SADNESS—OF PURIM

If we thought Judith was a problem, wait until we look at Esther! She involves us in issues that we don't usually think of in connection with women of God, as the title of this chapter may hint at.

Esther's story is at the very heart of the Jewish festival of Purim, the fourteenth of Adar. It is the most ebullient of celebrations. I learned this as a nine-year-old, when Ruthie, my best friend at school, invited me to celebrate Purim with her family. Well, I knew family celebrations, so I had a few doubts, but Ruthie was enthusiastic about the way her Hungarian Jewish family celebrated this feast. First of all, the kids got to make noise in *shul*, which (compared to the Hungarian Reformed Church, where kids were expected to maintain a petrified silence) sounded great to me. Every time the name Haman was mentioned we were not only *allowed* to make noise, we were *supposed* to. They would even give us noisemakers to help us along. Ruthie would get to wear the Queen Esther outfit her Auntie Ida had made for her, but it was OK, I didn't have to wear one. I could wear a funny mask if I wanted to, though.

To make the occasion even more fun, the adults would really be hilarious to watch. Her Uncle Morrie, the killjoy I'd met at the hardware store, would actually get drunk enough to get funny, and her grandfather, who was always so dignified, would *really* get snockered. It was Purim, she said—they were *supposed* to. (She admitted that the kids usually managed to sneak some of the kosher wine that Uncle Max brought from his store, and that was a lot of fun, too.)

Well, this sounded a lot like what happened at *any* holiday my family celebrated, though I had always gotten the distinct impression that my uncles weren't really *supposed* to get drunk. But what do kids know? But sure enough, dim and confused as my recollection of Purim was, I came away with the distinct impression that it was a holiday tailor-made for kids.

Something terrific had happened on that day, Ruthie told me. Some really wicked people wanted to kill all the Jews, but Queen Esther was so beautiful and so smart that she turned the tables on them and all the Jews were saved and the bad people, especially Haman, got what they deserved.

That was the only thing that confused me. This was 1949 and I lived in an Eastern European neighborhood. I already knew about the Holocaust, and that Queen Esther hadn't been around this time. It gave me a funny feeling. Sad. Terribly sad.

There really is something in Esther that's difficult to hear when you live in the beginning of the twenty-first century. Genocide is a word we see and hear too often, whether in the papers or in the memories of those for whom the dead are not statistics in the history books, but beloved faces never to be seen again. Because you can't read Esther without the idea rearing its head, and without asking where God was.

There are readers, too—Christians and Jews alike—who find the ending too bloodthirsty, as the Jews, saved from extermination by Esther's intervention, proceed to slaughter their enemies, down to the last woman and child. It's not something most of us can hear, even as fiction, without the images we've seen too often intruding themselves. I wish it wasn't in the book. I wish Esther had stopped with just saving her people. But she didn't, and they didn't, and we have to take it as it comes, the whole megillah.[13]

Having a slight problem with Esther isn't new. Esther wasn't actually accepted into the canon of the Jewish Scriptures until the third century C.E. It's not a work of history, but a kind of historical novella that dates from the early Hellenistic period. It's a decided oddity in that the word "God" never occurs in it, something that bothered later Greek-speaking Diaspora Jews enough that they made some additions to the Greek version of Esther (not the one actually used today in Jewish worship), which made them feel considerably better.

These additions give a more "religious" feel to the text, especially two long prayers in highly conventional religious language. They address some issues the original writer (and readers) of Esther found less problematic. For later readers, Esther and her uncle seemed too assimilated into the Persian culture in which the story is set. That issue had become increasingly painful and problematic to the Greek-speaking Jews of the Diaspora living in the Hellenistic world.

But again, taking Esther as it comes, it's not really a very old document, compared to stories like that of Sarah or Ruth—it wasn't part of the oral tradition. It's probably the work of a Diaspora Jew writing in the late fourth or early third century B.C.E., a well-educated writer, at that, obviously well acquainted with the ideas current in his time. Hence, in place of God, there's a shadowy hint of fate at work, an idea very popular in the Greek-influenced culture.

The writer sets the story in the court at Susa, the capital of Persia, in the time of King Xerxes I (Ahasuerus or Achashverosh), but he's probably not even remotely concerned with whether his readers believe the story is literally true or not. He embroiders and invents as he pleases, without trying to present an accurate picture of the court life of the time. He's a storyteller, not an historian, and expects that his readers know that, too.

THE KING OF KINGS AND HIS UPPITY QUEEN

To give him his due, the writer of the Book of Esther does tell an entertaining story. He opens with the scene at the court of Ahasuerus, King of Kings, in Susa, and gives us so minute a description of every facet of the court's furnishings he might be a stringer for *Architectural Digest*. The scene is opulent, luxurious, and when Ahasuerus throws a banquet for all his important officials, even the drinking goblets are described in close detail.

> *Drinking was by flagons, without restraint; for the king had given orders to all the officials of his palace to do as each one desired. Furthermore, Queen Vashti gave a banquet for the women in the palace of King Ahasuerus. (Esther 1:8–9)*

The men of the court are free to do as they please, since the presence of their wives won't cramp their style. Queen Vashti will be entertaining them. The banquet goes on for an amazing seven days (Esther 1:10), by which time we assume that everyone in the court is as hilarious as Ruthie's Uncle Morrie. At that point, impulsively, the king sends his eunuchs "to bring Queen Vashti before the king, wearing the royal crown, in order to show the peoples and the officials her beauty; for she was fair to behold. But Queen Vashti refused to come at the king's command conveyed by the eunuchs. At this the king was enraged, and his anger burned within him" (Esther 1:11–12). Queen Vashti has no doubt been aware of just what was going on at the king's banquet and showed pretty good sense, in my opinion, in not getting dressed up to parade in front of a drunken stag party.

He consults his sages to see what the law says about the queen's disobedience. One of them, Memucan, says,

> *"Not only has Queen Vashti done wrong to the king, but also to all the officials and all the peoples who are in all the provinces of King Ahasuerus. For this deed of the queen will be made known to all women, causing them to look with contempt on their husbands, since they will say, 'King Ahasuerus commanded Queen Vashti to be*

> *brought before him, and she did not come.' This very day the noble*
> *ladies of Persia and Media who have heard of the queen's behavior*
> *will rebel against the king's officials, and there will be no end of*
> *contempt and wrath!" (Esther 1:16–18)*

(It's been suggested that the writer of Esther knew contemporary "noble families" in real life, and fully expected to have women among his readers, or at least men who were married to wealthy, sophisticated wives.)

Memucan goes on to suggest the king pass a law forbidding Queen Vashti ever to appear before him again, strip her of her rank, and put another woman in her place. "So when the decree made by the king is proclaimed throughout all his kingdom, vast as it is, all women will give honor to their husbands, high and low alike" (Esther 1:20).

Needless to say, Ahasuerus likes the plan a lot. Queen Vashti is stripped of her rank and forbidden ever to come before the king again. There's nothing in the text to indicate how Vashti took this, but she may not have been exactly heartbroken. (In case you're wondering, she was no doubt a woman from another royal household, who could certainly not be killed or imprisoned without offending her kin. She got to retire to a comfortable life within the court, though she'd no longer be queen or chief wife.)

Finally, Ahasuerus sends letters out to the entire kingdom, "declaring that every man should be master in his own house" (Esther 1:22). No doubt the original readers thought this was vastly amusing, which does tell us something.

THE GREAT VIRGIN ROUNDUP

Now that Queen Vashti is history, the king is encouraged to send out and round up every eligible virgin available and bring them to Susa, so that the king can pick the one that pleases him the most to be queen (Esther 2:2–4). Clearly, this is fiction: royal marriages were state matters involving treaties, trading rights, properties, advantageous alliances, and military aid. But rounding up beautiful girls would have sounded like more fun to the storyteller's readers.

We are now introduced to Mordecai (Mordechai), a fourth-generation Jewish exile, who has risen to a position of responsibility in the court. (In fact, the first group of exiles from Jerusalem were drawn almost exclusively from the wealthy and educated classes, the ruling classes, as a way of making sure the Jews left behind did not have leaders. Most of them soon occupied civil service positions in exile similar to the ones they had occupied at home. They were scribes, accountants, tax collectors, archivists, and so on.) Mordecai has raised a young cousin, Esther (Hadassah), who had been orphaned at an early age, and adopted her as his daughter (Esther 2:5–7).

Esther, a beautiful unmarried woman, is promptly taken off to the king's harem and placed in the custody of Hegai, the eunuch in charge of the virgins being prepared for the king. "The girl pleased him and won his favor, and he quickly provided her with her cosmetic treatments and her portion of food, and with seven chosen maids from the king's palace, and advanced her and her maids to the best place in the harem" (Esther 2:9). This is one of the points that was fine with the original audience, but disturbed later readers. Apparently, Esther happily eats whatever food is given to her at the court, unlike Judith, who is scrupulous about following the prescribed dietary laws.

Esther did not reveal her people or kindred, for Mordecai had charged
her not to tell. Every day Mordecai would walk around in front of the
court of the harem, to learn how Esther was and how she fared.
(Esther 2:10–11)

There is in fact no reason why Esther's identity as a Jew would have been a problem. It would not have been, at the royal Persian court, which had been accustomed to having Jews around for several generations. The Persians were a cosmopolitan people who were used to seeing people of different religions in the capital city, which was a major trading center. The secrecy, however, is necessary for the purpose of building tension in the story; it is a surprise that will be sprung later.

The writer even gives us a fair description of the elaborate beauty treatments all the young women are given: "Six months with oil of myrrh and six months with perfumes and cosmetics for women" (Esther 2:12). (Why cosmetics "for women"? Cosmetics were for men as well at the Persian court, where eye makeup and perfumes were common. It's one of the reasons why Alexander's Macedonians were originally so scornful of the conquered Persians.)

Each virgin is prepared, then sent along to the king on her appointed evening. In the morning she is sent to the second harem, the one for women who are no longer virgins. The narrator wants us to understand that even in this situation, Esther is a cut above the other young women. Each is permitted to take with her anything she pleases, but Esther ". . . asked for nothing except what Hegai the king's eunuch, who had charge of the women, advised. Now Esther was admired by all who saw her" (Esther 2:15).

No one will be surprised, of course, when the king instantly decides that Esther is the one and makes her Queen of Persia. "[S]he won his favor and devotion, so that he set the royal crown on her head and made her queen instead of Vashti. Then the king gave a great banquet to all his officials and ministers—'Esther's banquet.' He also granted a holiday to the provinces, and gave gifts with royal liberality" (Esther 2:17–18).

The narrator now presents a flashback, dating back to when Esther first came to the harem as a virgin (yes, right, that's why I said the term "the whole

megillah" was ironically applied to Esther: it wanders). Mordecai uncovers a
plot to assassinate the king and passes the word along to Esther. Esther,
without revealing who she really is or what her relationship to Mordecai is,
passes the plot on to the king, in Mordecai's name. The conspirators are
hanged, and "it was recorded in the book of the annals in the presence of the
king" (Esther 2:23). This seems like an odd and unrelated little episode, but
the author is preparing a surprise for later.

ENTER THE VILLAIN

After these things King Ahasuerus promoted Haman son of
Hammedatha the Agagite, and advanced him and set his seat above
all the officials who were with him. And all the king's servants who
were at the king's gate bowed down and did obeisance to Haman;
for the king had so commanded concerning him.
But Mordecai did not bow down or do obeisance. (Esther 3:1–2)

Mordecai, questioned by the king's servants, exempts himself because he
is a Jew (and presumably would not bow down before any but his god). A
little explanation is needed here. The bow in question is not just a polite little
nip-at-the-waist sort of affair; the writer is talking about a royal obeisance,
which in Persia meant a full prostration. It was actually reserved for the king
and the gods. Haman is incensed,

But he thought it beneath him to lay hands on Mordecai alone. So,
having been told who Mordecai's people were, Haman plotted to
destroy all the Jews, the people of Mordecai, throughout the whole
kingdom of Ahasuerus. In the first month, which is the month of
Nisan, in the twelfth year of King Ahasuerus, they cast Pur—which
means "the lot"—before Haman for the day and for the month,
and the lot fell on the thirteenth day of the twelfth month,
which is the month of Adar. (Esther 3:6–7)

(This is the explanation for why the feast will hereafter be called Purim.)

Then Haman said to King Ahasuerus, "There is a certain people
scattered and separated among the peoples in all the provinces of
your kingdom; their laws are different from those of every other
people, and they do not keep the king's laws, so that it is not
appropriate for the king to tolerate them." (Esther 3:8)

Haman urges the king to issue a decree to have all the Jews destroyed. He
is deliberately lying here, but since he sweetens the pot by offering to put up
10,000 talents of silver to have the decree carried out, the king (who does not

seem to be the brightest of all rulers who ever sat on the throne of Persia) agrees happily.

> *Letters were sent by couriers to all the king's provinces, giving orders*
> *to destroy, to kill, and to annihilate all Jews, young and old, women*
> *and children, in one day, the thirteenth day of the twelfth month,*
> *which is the month of Adar, and to plunder their goods. A copy of the*
> *document was to be issued as a decree in every province by*
> *proclamation, calling on all the peoples to be ready for that day.*
> *(Esther 3:13–14)*

Presumably, the Jews living throughout the Persian Empire will simply wait for the date.

There is great mourning among the Jews of Susa, and Mordecai dresses himself in sackcloth and goes to the palace. Since he cannot enter the palace in his sackcloth, and Esther (now the Queen), cannot go out to him, she sends a eunuch to find out what's happening, and Mordecai relays the news to Esther, begging her ". . . to go to the king to make supplication to him and entreat him for her people" (Esther 4:8).

Esther responds:

> *"All the king's servants and the people of the king's provinces know*
> *that if any man or woman goes to the king inside the inner court*
> *without being called, there is but one law—all alike are to be put to*
> *death. Only if the king holds out the golden scepter to someone, may*
> *that person live. I myself have not been called to come in to the king*
> *for thirty days." (Esther 4:11)*

(This is a complete fiction, of course, but without it the dramatic narrative would lose most of its tension.)

> *Mordecai told them to reply to Esther, "Do not think that in the*
> *king's palace you will escape any more than all the other Jews. For if*
> *you keep silence at such a time as this, relief and deliverance will rise*
> *for the Jews from another quarter, but you and your father's family*
> *will perish. Who knows? Perhaps you have come to royal dignity for*
> *just such a time as this." (Esther 4:13–14)*

THE TRANSFORMATION OF ESTHER

Up until now, Esther has been little more than a cardboard figure, a puppet. She has obeyed Mordecai in everything, up to going into the harem and not telling anyone who she is. She has obeyed the eunuch Hegai and become a favorite. Presumably she has pleased the king who, as we have seen, has no use for independent women. We have seen nothing of her personality; in fact all we really know of her is that she is beautiful.

But all this changes with Mordecai's speech.

He reminds her that merely being in the palace will not save her: she is still a Jew. If she keeps silence, she will surely perish. Note that odd line: "relief and deliverance will rise for the Jews from another quarter." We still have no real hint of God acting here, but Mordecai hints that perhaps her being chosen queen was fated, to serve at just this moment.

The obedient young girl suddenly issues an astonishing directive to her uncle:

> "Go, gather all the Jews to be found in Susa, and hold a fast on my behalf, and neither eat nor drink for three days, night or day. I and my maids will also fast as you do. After that I will go to the king, though it is against the law; and if I perish, I perish." (Esther 4:16)

Now she is not doing as others tell her: it is Esther who is suddenly issuing the commands. This is an astonishing reversal, because up until now we have been given no hint whatever that she is capable of exercising authority, much less of devising the sly and masterful plan she will unfold. "If I perish, I perish." These are not the words of the soft young woman she has been up till now. Esther is coming into her queenhood in a truly regal fashion.

On the third day, Esther, carefully prepared, goes to the court. Neither she nor the audience knows whether she will live or die: she is entirely alone here. But the king, pleased with her, beckons her to approach. The readers heave a collective sigh. Esther's life is spared. It remains to be seen whether the life of the Jews of Persia will be spared.

At this point, we have no idea what Esther plans to do to save the Jews. The king willingly offers to give her anything she wants, up to half of his kingdom (Esther 5:3). Will she ask him to spare the Jews?

But no. Esther merely says, "If it pleases the king, let the king and Haman come today to a banquet that I have prepared for the king" (Esther 5:4).

The reader is puzzled at first. What now? The king quickly agrees, and he and Haman go to dine with Esther. A second time, he asks her for her petition; he will give her everything up to half his kingdom (Esther 5:6).

Will she ask now?

No, again Esther temporizes. If the king and Haman will come to the banquet she will give the next night, then she will tell him what she wants (Esther 5:8).

Obviously, Esther is up to something, for which the feast is simply some kind of scene-setting. What that consists of starts to be hinted at in the next scene, when we see the delight with which Haman receives the news.

However, he passes Mordecai sitting in the gate, and he is once more overwhelmed by fury. The narrator may wander, but this piece, at least, is well crafted. We begin to get the feeling that Haman is being set up.

Haman, a man very full of himself, calls all of his friends and proceeds to brag about his wealth, his sons, the honors the king gives him, and the fact that only he, besides the king, has been the guest at Esther's banquet that night, and will be again tomorrow. "Yet all this does me no good so long as I see the Jew Mordecai sitting at the king's gate," he concludes (Esther 5:13).

Then his wife Zeresh and all his friends said to him, "Let a gallows fifty cubits high be made, and in the morning tell the king to have Mordecai hanged on it; then go with the king to the banquet in good spirits." This advice pleased Haman, and he had the gallows made.
(Esther 5:14)

THE TABLES BEGIN TO TURN

"On that night the king could not sleep, and he gave orders to bring the book of records, the annals, and they were read to the king" (Esther 6:1). Good plan. If there is anything that could put a person to sleep, having an official read you the transcript of the royal records would do it!

The king hears the account of Mordecai's part in unmasking the conspiracy to kill the king and asks what has been done to honor him for this. Nothing, he is told.

There follows one of the slyest and most delicious scenes in the Scriptures.

The king said, "Who is in the court?" Now Haman had just entered the outer court of the king's palace to speak to the king about having Mordecai hanged on the gallows that he had prepared for him. So the king's servants told him, "Haman is there, standing in the court." The king said, "Let him come in." So Haman came in, and the king said to him, "What shall be done for the man whom the king wishes to honor?" Haman said to himself, "Whom would the king wish to honor more than me?" (Esther 6:4–6)

Positively rubbing his hands with delight, Haman outlines exactly the highest honors he would like the king to pay to him. Let the royal robes be put on the man, Haman says, and let him be mounted on one of the king's own horses, with a crown on its head. One of the king's highest officials shall then lead the horse through the streets proclaiming before him: "Thus shall it be done for the man whom the king wishes to honor" (Esther 6:9).

The full joke is now sprung on Haman:

*Then the king said to Haman, "Quickly, take the robes and the horse,
as you have said, and do so to the Jew Mordecai who sits at the king's
gate. Leave out nothing that you have mentioned." So Haman took
the robes and the horse and robed Mordecai and led him riding
through the open square of the city, proclaiming, "Thus shall it be
done for the man whom the king wishes to honor." (Esther 6:10–11)*

Haman, who has just built a gallows to hang Mordecai on, finds himself having to conduct his hated enemy through the streets, a mere flunky assigned to honoring someone in the king's name. Mortified and angry, he returns home, where his wife tells him: "If Mordecai, before whom your downfall has begun, is of the Jewish people, you will not prevail against him, but will surely fall before him" (Esther 6:13).

It is with this grim little prophecy that Haman goes off to Esther's second banquet, where the trap has been baited and prepared. The king asks a third time what Esther's petition is, and this time she answers him:

*"If I have won your favor, O king, and if it pleases the king, let my life
be given me—that is my petition—and the lives of my people—that
is my request. For we have been sold, I and my people, to be
destroyed, to be killed, and to be annihilated. If we had been sold
merely as slaves, men and women, I would have held my peace; but
no enemy can compensate for this damage to the king."
(Esther 7:3–4)*

Esther has learned something in court life, it seems. Note that she ends her plea with an appeal to the king's vanity (or dignity; it's truly hard to tell, with Ahasuerus, which is which). Merely selling her people as slaves would not make her ask, "but no enemy can compensate for this damage to the king."

*Then King Ahasuerus said to Queen Esther, "Who is he, and where is
he, who has presumed to do this?" Esther said, "a foe and enemy, this
wicked Haman!" Then Haman was terrified before the king
and the queen. (Esther 7:5–6)*

Well, that's done it!

The king is so furious and distracted that he goes out into the garden to cool off; meanwhile Haman throws himself on Esther's couch (where she is reclining to dine). In a final horrid bit of comedy, the king comes in and sees Haman half-lying on Esther's couch and exclaims: "'Will he even assault the queen in my presence, in my own house?' As the words left the mouth of the king, they covered Haman's face" (Esther 7:8). (In other words, Haman has already ceased to exist.)

The final insult is yet to come:

Then Harbona, one of the eunuchs in attendance on the king, said,
"Look, the very gallows that Haman has prepared for Mordecai,
whose word saved the king, stands at Haman's house, fifty cubits
high." And the king said, "Hang him on that." So they hanged
Haman on the gallows that he had prepared for Mordecai.
Then the anger of the king abated. (Esther 7:9–10)

GENOCIDE REVERSED

Esther is given Haman's property and Mordecai his position, but that merely rewards them for unmasking the awful plot. Esther now seeks to save her people from the orders that have already been sent out. The king (as if you haven't guessed that he's about as sharp as a tofu cube) replies, "You may write as you please with regard to the Jews, in the name of the king, and seal it with the king's ring; for an edict written in the name of the king and sealed with the king's ring cannot be revoked" (Esther 8:8). He has just given Esther and Mordecai *carte blanche*; they can do anything they like and it will be irrevocable. Notice, moreover, that he has given the signet to Esther, not to Mordecai, who is now the highest official in Susa.

It is Mordecai, however, who dictates the actual edict. In the king's name, the Jews of each city are permitted not only to defend themselves, but ". . . to destroy, to kill, and to annihilate any armed force of any people or province that might attack them, with their children and women, and to plunder their goods on a single day throughout all the provinces of King Ahasuerus, on the thirteenth day of the twelfth month, which is the month of Adar" (Esther 8:11–12). Esther is clearly behind the scenes here.

All the officials of the provinces, the satraps and the governors, and
the royal officials were supporting the Jews, because the fear of
Mordecai had fallen upon them. For Mordecai was powerful in the
king's house, and his fame spread throughout all the provinces as the
man Mordecai grew more and more powerful. (Esther 9:3–4)

He is the public figure; Esther is behind the scenes, at least as far as the government officials are concerned.

There follows a distressing account of the slaughter: "So the Jews struck down all their enemies with the sword, slaughtering, and destroying them, and did as they pleased to those who hated them" (Esther 9:5). Esther requests a second day of slaughter, to allow the Jews of Susa to share in the victory and to kill Haman's sons along with their other enemies.

Esther has come very far: she has gone from obedient adopted daughter and submissive queen to a woman risking her life to save her people, and doing it with almost diabolical cleverness. Next, she has shown herself to be anything but gentle in seeking revenge on the enemies of her people. Finally, she reaches the fullest part of her authority: it is Esther who authorizes the annual celebration of Purim to commemorate the victory over their enemies (Esther 9:26–32). It ends with: "The command of Queen Esther fixed these practices of Purim, and it was recorded in writing" (Esther 9:32).

This, you realize, makes Esther the only woman who actually institutes and authorizes a religious holiday. The narrator, however, is careful to end the book by noting that Mordecai was next in rank to the king, which is reminiscent of the ending of Judith, in which she is suddenly back to being the widow of "Manasseh her husband."

After all, the storyteller seems to be saying, this *is* a work of fiction.

HELEN'S STORY

I've heard a lot of other women's stories, and I think this one may be one of the harder ones to hear, but some stories are just hard. Period. I think my mother and my Aunt Lena had that kind of story. I probably don't have to say any more than to tell you that they were Jewish, and lived in Germany, and it was the 1930s.

Actually, it's more complicated than that. My mother's family was Jewish, but they were not religious. Not at all. You'd call them sophisticated people, cosmopolitan. Aunt Lena and her mother went to the opera and the ballet, not the synagogue. They went to Paris to get their dresses, and to Switzerland to go skiing. They took a cruise every year—maybe to New York, maybe to South America. Even in the Depression, they had that kind of money. Aunt Lena was a real glamour girl who made what was considered a very good match, a man whose family went back to God-knows-when, real aristocracy. The fact that she was Jewish and he wasn't didn't matter all that much to anybody in their circle at that point. These were very sophisticated people, who thought Hitler was some kind of comic-opera madman. Were they in for a surprise!

My mother was a change-of-life baby, eighteen years younger than Aunt Lena. She was really young enough to be Aunt Lena's daughter instead of her sister. Which was probably a good thing, as it turned out.

I don't need to tell you what happened to the German Jews when Hitler came to power. People like my mother's family lost their rights, then their businesses and their money, and finally their lives. But people like Aunt Lena were often able to survive pretty well. She was married to an Aryan, and she and her husband moved in a social circle where they knew a lot of important people. I don't suppose anyone really thought of her as Jewish.

When my mother was nine, my grandparents asked Aunt Lena to look after her for a few days, just while they were visiting a friend in Munich who thought he could get them out of Germany. It was a good thing they asked her, because they never actually made it to Munich. God knows when or where or how they died. But they were gone. For Aunt Lena it was a shock she really wasn't ready for. She and her husband—like a lot of people—just didn't want to know what was happening, and they certainly didn't want to find themselves involved in anything that would make life unpleasant for them. One thing Aunt Lena's husband was very clear about: nobody must know that she and her little sister were Jewish.

Well, we're not all born to be heroes, and Aunt Lena had probably never made a harder decision than choosing what hat to wear with her new outfit. She didn't even try to go against what her husband told her. So life went along exactly like it had before, except that she and her husband had this extra little "daughter." They went to dinners and plays, they gave their daughters dancing lessons and piano lessons, and they went for picnics on Sundays. It's almost crazy to think that things this normal were going on while millions of people were dying, but it's true.

Finally, Aunt Lena approached an old Jewish man her parents had known, to see if there was something she could do to help the Jews, and he told her, "You made your choice. It's too late for you to be a Jew." His contempt crushed her.

Those two poor unhappy women! Aunt Lena couldn't be who she was, and my mother didn't even know who she was. She only knew she was never, never supposed to talk about her parents, or tell anyone where she lived before, or what her real name was. She was like the little girl who never was. But they survived.

Survivor's guilt is a funny thing. There's my mother, who still feels guilty that when other children were dying in Auschwitz, she was being taken to piano lessons in a chauffeur-driven Daimler, and what did she do with her life? She became a child psychologist, a therapist, working with kids who sometimes had unbearable guilt and shame. And Aunt Lena, what did she become? A Jew! Would you believe it? A real Jew. Not only a Jew, but she moved to Israel years later and spent the rest of her life there! Like she told my mother once, "That old man was wrong. It's never too late to be a Jew. It's never too late to be anything, if you want it enough." I guess she wanted it enough.

I know, it's not much like Esther's story, is it? Aunt Lena didn't defy Hitler, or even her husband. She didn't save her people. She only saved one little girl she didn't have any choice about saving. But she saved her all the same, and I like to think that, in a way, she saved herself, too, when she decided to become a real Jew in the end.

She was a very unorthodox *Jewish aunt, I guess, but she taught me something that even an orthodox aunt wouldn't disagree with, something that has made all the difference in my own life. You know what it is?*

It's never too late with God. *Never. Blessed be the Name.*

QUESTIONS FOR STUDY AND REFLECTION
In reading the story:
- What does the narrative tell us about Esther?
- How does she change or grow during the course of the story?
- What can you tell about her relationship with God?
- What kind of courage does she show compared to, say, Judith?

Self-reflection and learning:
- Can I identify with this woman?
- Is she a person I can admire or emulate?
- What parts of Esther do I want to own? Disown?
- What troubling questions does she raise for me?

What questions and problems does this still leave unanswered or "in process"?

CHAPTER NINE

Our Lives, Our Stories: Being God's Women Today

THE POWER OF STORIES

Granted, very few of us have stories cut on quite as epic a scale as Judith's; almost none of us are married to the same man our sister wed. Frankly, I don't know a single person who claims to have had a face-to-face, one-on-one meeting with God at a well in the wilderness. Most of us, in fact, probably suspect our stories are too modest to make even the local headlines (come to think of it, we probably *hope* that's true!), much less be canonized and handed down through the centuries. Our stories, we fear, are far too dull to interest anyone but us.

Now that I reflect on it, it's likely that the women whose stories we've seen in these pages would have been astonished to know that, thousands of years down the road, men and women they didn't know, speaking languages they never heard, and living in a world they couldn't even imagine, were still telling these stories. I can almost hear my grandmother or one of my aunts saying, "Oh, my God! You're *not* going to tell them about the time I . . . ." Probably these Old Testament women would have said the same thing: "You're not *really* going to tell them about the time I gave those mandrakes to my sister Rachel, are you? We were so young then, and it all seemed so important." "Oh, no! *Don't* tell them how I planned things out for Ruth and Boaz! What would people think of me?"

But aren't we glad that someone told?

Like us, most of the women whose stories we've heard probably saw only the everyday in which the big stories were embedded, the days that went on like every other day, filled with everyday concerns like little Levi's cough, and everyday activities like bending over in the field or at the washing place in the river.

But there's power in stories, and that's exactly what this book is about. The stories we've seen, even with all the distortions, mistranslations, and misinterpretations that have crept in over the centuries—even with large chunks of them missing and huge questions left unanswered—still have the power to lift us, stir us, throw a startling and clarifying light on our own lives. And these stories have this power even though they're thousands of years old, about women whose lives aren't remotely like the ones we lead today. How much more powerful are some of the living stories we have heard in voices closer to our own day!

GIFTS IN EVERYDAY WRAPPING

Years ago, at a vestry retreat, when the group members were telling their stories to one another, my friend Shirley Webb said something that's stuck with me ever since. She said hearing another person's story is like unwrapping a surprise package and discovering a wonderful gift inside. "Now that I've heard your story," she said, "how can I not love you?"

Now that I've heard your story, how can I not love you? How can I not understand what an achievement the most ordinary day of your life is? How can I not be surprised at the gift your story holds for me?

Shirley Webb was right. In all my years of listening to stories, I've heard plenty of them that moved me as deeply, struck me as forcefully, and opened my eyes as astonishingly as the ones in these pages, even though they were told in flat, everyday voices that still told me that the teller grew up in rural Tennessee or still couldn't manage the grammar of this language she didn't learn till she was thirty. No matter. The story shone through, a gift in the everyday wrapping.

Then, too, there were the stories that astonished me because I saw the seamed, ninety-year-old face of the teller, worn with nearly a century of cares, and heard in her voice the breathless excitement of the seventeen-year-old girl on her way to her first dance, and I suddenly realized, "My God! She's still alive in there!"—and what's more, I could *see* her!

Yes, there's more than power in stories. There's a profound magic that can suspend time, bring back forgotten voices, and make the dead live, breathe, and even dance again.

But I regret one thing about all these stories I've heard: seldom have I told anyone how long their story has stayed with me, or how often its strength, wisdom, or humor has come to my rescue over the years. Seldom have I thanked God for these, the richest of all spiritual treasures that nurture me.

And that's something we all need to understand.

BEING WOMEN OF GOD TODAY

These women of God, whose stories we've seen, have done more than share their small triumphs and everyday agonies. Woven in and through their lives and stories are the most profound insights into the very heart of life itself: the story that God is weaving with us. Now shown on the grand scale, as the heavenly visitor appearing unexpectedly in the wilderness, now unseen in the heat of conflict or the grief of loss, God has been the constant presence whose breath animates the very lives lived out in these pages. God has been the grand storyteller, the lofty author of our days. And yes, God has also been the silent companion who's heard the sometimes faltering words in which ordinary women tried to explain who they were and why they lived as they did.

This is the incredible gift of the Scriptures. Who would have known, seen, caught the ever-growing understanding of God's compassion if someone hadn't told the story, however well or poorly they were able? We're the People of the Book, and therefore we're People of the Story. The three great monotheistic traditions whose stories weave in and out of these pages can only exist today because someone preserved and told the stories and repeated the words.

Granted, when we turn to the Bible on our shelves, the stories we find have often been distorted, and parts of them have disappeared entirely. True, the voices we hear most often in the text are the voices of men who wrote without understanding the depth or the importance of the stories they heard from the women who told them. They loved Grandma, of course, but her story couldn't *possibly* be as important as the royal archives or the list of men who governed the country. But the stories stuck to the pages anyway, thanks be to God, and we are the richer for them.

What does this mean to us? Telling our own stories is not simply a way of passing on amusing little anecdotes or family traditions. Telling our stories is a ministry, a calling, a mission entrusted to us, because no one else can fulfill it. God gave us the power to work this profound and everyday magic as others have worked it for us, to send gifts in humble wrappings down to the children who will not be born until we have left. And each re-telling, each new thread added, will make the whole fabric of God's story richer.

If we can't be a Sarah, we can be a Nancy, surprised into laughter by God's sudden touch of grace in an A.A. meeting. If we can't tell the story of Naomi, we can be a Helen, holding fast to the God with whom it's never too late. These are all ways in which we add to the story, so that the text on the shelf will be kept alive, too, even when we no longer add to the written words within it.

The earthiness and humor of these women's stories, adhering slyly to the grander biblical saga, have kept the text alive and fresh for us. Our own stories, too, infuse fresh life into the story of this strange and unexpected God who ignores the obvious, sides with the unfavored, and blesses even those who are doing their best to get in the way of things.

In other words, the story is far from over, and it won't be over as long as new voices—yours and mine and the woman at the checkout stand—go on telling stories. They may not be as impressive as the ones that Hollywood tells us, or as nice as the ones we heard in Sunday School. But the real stories are never really like that, anyway. God's women are, above all, *real* people. Living with God, how could they be otherwise?

APPENDIX ONE

Some Tips for Study Group Leaders

GOD OF OUR MOTHERS AS A CLASS

God of Our Mothers was originally designed as a class to be taught in parishes. Hence it tries for an informal approach to Scripture rather than a scholarly one, an approach that will invite women (and men) to enter into the spirit of the stories. While it can certainly stand on its own for a single reader, these brief study tips are designed for parish leaders who'd like to present this as a class or study group. In Appendix 2, we've also provided some reflection questions and biblical story outlines to hand out as study aids, whether you're studying this book, or simply the scriptural readings themselves. The focus in the book is always on adult readers and learners, but that's a pretty wide group.

In its simplest form, each weekly, biweekly, or monthly class would cover one chapter. This would mean the chapter and the scriptural reading that goes with it. Keep in mind that for many people, this is more reading than they may want to do. Never press people to think they *must* read it all! Have the students bring their books and Bibles to class so they can refer to them during the class. This is critical, especially if you want to invite new folks in along the way, or retain students who have to miss one or more classes. Assure people that they'll pick up enough of the story so they will not feel lost. And honor that promise!

Appendix 2 contains handout materials for the classes, consisting of Scripture outlines and some study and reflection questions. Concentrate most on the reflections, which suggest questions for the students to ask themselves about the readings. This should be a lively forum for discussion, not a deadly "study group."

One or two people per week may be asked to open and close the group

151

with a poem, a prayer, some music, or something that reminds them of the readings. See if someone will volunteer to tell a real-life story for each class. Above all, ask for stories! That is the heart of this book, and if you can get students thinking about the stories of real people they know, which reflect the themes found in the Scripture, then the book has done its job. It's not about training Bible scholars, but opening people's eyes to the lively stories that still speak to us in the pages of Scripture.

Feel free to pick and choose! There's a lot of material here. Do a short class with only two or three stories. Chose one or two stories for a weekend retreat, which would give people lots of time to read, reflect, and share. Ask participants to do the readings before they arrive, if possible, to leave more time for reflection and deepening the stories.

Keep it going! Nothing says you have to do a chapter every week. Do the chapter. Next week, read the Scripture aloud together (maybe from a different translation) and discuss it. Next week, have people come back and tell their stories. Encourage people to record them, write them down, illustrate them, bring in mementoes and photos of the people involved, so that everyone can see what Grandma Anne looked like or where exactly in Mexico *Abuelita Juana* came from.

For a weekend retreat, or on the last night of a class, invite people to bring pictures, mementoes, or tokens of the women of God in their lives and create a table or "altar" to display them—complete with candles and flowers, and so on. Schedule some sharing time for each participant to show what they've brought and why, and to tell how this particular woman's life touched them on their own spiritual and life journey.

Granted, this is all fairly nebulous, but groups differ so much, and congregational cultures differ so much, that it's easier to throw out some general suggestions and trust the people who know their groups the best to come up with a plan for presenting this material.

One thing is certain, though: stories in and of themselves fascinate people, and it often doesn't take any more than that to make a lively and engaging class.

APPENDIX TWO

Study Guide Materials

The following materials are intended to be handed out for use in study groups, workshops, or retreats. For each chapter, you will find two handouts:

- An overview page that lists the chapters, verses, and themes
- A reflections page that suggests some questions to ponder or discuss

It's best to give these pages out well in advance of class meetings, for use as reading guides. Use good-sized type and bright colors on regular-sized paper, and allow for plenty of room for taking notes. (I have become notorious, among my students, for putting things on the most garish colors I can find. Anything that keeps things from getting lost on your desk.) The sheets might even be put in a binder and handed out all together at the beginning of the class.

CHAPTER 1
STILL FRIENDS WITH GOD: THE EVE NO ONE REMEMBERS
The Creation Stories
(Genesis 1:1–5:2)

First Creation Story
(Genesis 1:1–2:4a)
1:1–24   First six days of creation
1:25   Humankind created
2:1–4a   The Sabbath

Second Creation Story
    (Genesis 2:4b–4:25)

2:4b	Second creation story begins
2:7	Creation of man
2:8–17	Eden created; tree of knowledge of good and evil forbidden
2:18–20	The great helpmeet search
2:21	Creation of woman
3:1–11	Temptation and fall
3:12–21	Confrontation with God; exile from Eden
4:1	Birth of Cain and Abel
4:2–24	Cain's Story
4:25	Birth of Seth

First Creation Story Continued
    (Genesis 5:1–2)

5:1–2	First creation story continued from 2:4a

REFLECTIONS ON CHAPTER 1
    In reading the story:
- What *doesn't* the narrative say that I expect it to say?
- What does the narrative tell me that I *don't* expect?
- What does the *story* actually tell me about Eve?
- What is her relationship with God at the start of the story?
- Where is she at the end of the story?

    Self-reflection and learning:
- Where in my life do I resemble her?
- Have I had an "eye-opening" I can identify in my life?
- What can I learn from her?
- What light does this story throw on my own?

What questions and problems does this still leave unanswered or "in process"?

CHAPTER 2
FAMILY VALUES IN ABRAHAM, OR ". . . AND BABY MAKES FOUR"
    The Abraham Saga
        (Genesis 12–25)

    Sarah
        (Genesis 16–18:15; 21:1–14)

12	First promise, first danger
12:10	The danger in Egypt
13:14	Second promise
14	Interlude for war
15	Third promise
16	The struggle begins
17	Covenant and circumcision
18	The heavenly visitors
18–20	(Sodom and Gomorrah interlude)
20	The second danger
21	Birth of Isaac
23	Death of Sarah
25	Abraham's other sons

REFLECTIONS ON CHAPTER 2

In reading the story:
- What does the narrative tell us about this woman? Her position? Problems and desires? Personality?
- What makes her tick?
- What strengths does she have? What flaws?
- What is her relationship with God like?
- Where is she at the end of the story?

Self-reflection and learning:
- Where in my life do I resemble her?
- How have I dealt with problems in ways similar to hers?
- What can I learn from her, either good or bad?
- Has someone else played "Sarah" in my life?

What questions and problems does this still leave unanswered or "in process"?

CHAPTER 3
"THE MOTHER OF ALL BELIEVERS": HAGAR'S JOURNEY TO FREEDOM
The Abraham Saga
(Genesis 12–25)

Hagar
(Genesis 16–18:15; 21:1–20)

16	The struggle begins
17	Covenant and circumcision
18	The heavenly visitors
21	Birth of Isaac

| 20–21 | Hagar's journey |
| 25 | Burial by Isaac and Ishmael |

REFLECTIONS ON CHAPTER 3

In reading the story:
- What is Hagar's position? Problems and desires? Personality?
- What makes her tick?
- What strengths does she have? What flaws?
- What is her relationship with God at the start of the story?
- How does this relationship appear to develop?
- Where is she at the end of the story?

Self-reflection and learning:
- What in my life has resembled Hagar's?
- How have I dealt with problems in ways similar to hers?
- What light does she throw on my own story?
- Has someone else played Hagar in my life?
- How have Hagar's "three gifts" worked in my life?

What questions and problems does this still leave unanswered or "in process"?

CHAPTER 4

THE INVISIBLE MAN AND THE MANAGING WOMAN, OR "MOTHER KNOWS BEST"

The Rebekah Story
   (Genesis 22–27)

22	Isaac: The Invisible Man
23	The death of Sarah
24	A wife for Isaac
24:15	Rebekah: not your usual "nice girl"
25:21	Another barren woman
25:28	Mama's boy and Daddy's boy
26:6–11	Third danger
27:1–17	Rebekah bends tradition
27:42–46	The last word

REFLECTIONS ON CHAPTER 4

In reading the story:
- What do her actions tell us about Rebekah? Her family?
- How does she deal with expectations? Customs?
- Is she a good match for Isaac?

- What strengths does she have? What flaws?
- How well does she understand her family?
- How does God "make use" of Rebekah?

Self-reflection and learning:
- Where in my life do I resemble Rebekah?
- Have I dealt with restrictions and frustrations in similar ways? Different ways?
- What can I learn from her, either good or bad?
- What light does this throw on my own story?

What questions and problems does this still leave unanswered or "in process"?

CHAPTER 5
"SISTERS, SISTERS . . .": SIBLING RIVALRY TO THE MAX
Rachel and Leah
(Genesis 28:1 through 31:32)

28:1	Rebekah's plan unfolds
29:4–11	Another meeting at a well
29:13–30	Setting up the scene
29:32–35	God chooses sides (?)
30:5–24	The competition
30:25–43	Another competition
31:1–32	The parting of the ways
35:16	Competing to the end

REFLECTIONS ON CHAPTER 5
In reading the story:
- What does the narrative tell us about the sisters' personalities?
- What does their relationship tell us?
- Who "wins" the competition? Who "loses"?
- How do they involve others in their story?
- Where are they by the end of the story?

Self-reflection and learning:
- Have I been part of a Leah-and-Rachel competition in my life?
- Who do I identify with more: Leah or Rachel?
- Where in my life have I been like them?
- Have I been able to do things differently than they did?

What questions and problems does this still leave unanswered or "in process"?

CHAPTER 6

RUTH AND NAOMI: "GETTING BY WITH A LITTLE HELP FROM OUR FRIENDS"

The Book of Ruth (entire text)

1:1–7	Separation and exile
1:8–14	Naomi's bitterness
1:16–17	Ruth's faithfulness
2:1–3	Working to survive
2:4–7	Enter Boaz
2:8–16	The plot thickens
3:1–5	Naomi's sneaky plan
4:1–6	Boaz's sneaky plan
4:14–17	Full repatriation
4:18–21	Ruth, ancestress of kings

(*see also* Matthew 1:1–17)

REFLECTIONS ON CHAPTER 6

In reading the story:
- What does the narrative tell us about Ruth and Naomi's personalities?
- What does their relationship tell us?
- What might be called unusual about them?
- What strengths do each of them have?
- How do they use their strengths for each other's benefit?
- Where are they by the end of the story?

Self-reflection and learning:
- Do I have a Ruth or Naomi in my life?
- Where in my life am I like Naomi? Ruth?
- How do my own strengths and weaknesses work together?
- What light does this throw on my own story?

What questions and problems does this still leave unanswered or "in process"?

CHAPTER 7

JUDITH: THE WOMAN AND THE WARRIOR

The Book of Judith (Skip Chapters 1–6)

7:10–32	Bethuliah under siege
8:1–8	Introducing Judith
8:9–36	Judith's speech
9	Judith's prayer
10:1–23	Judith goes to meet the enemy
11	Judith's speech to Holofernes
12	Judith's plan unfolds

13	The murder of Holofernes
14–15	Bethuliah and Jerusalem delivered
16:1–17	The song of Judith
16:21–25	Honoring Judith

REFLECTIONS ON CHAPTER 7

In reading the story:
- What does the narrative tell us about Judith's social position?
- What do we learn about her picture of God?
- What kind of courage does she exhibit? What kind of craftiness?
- What do you think of the honors paid her?

Self-reflection and learning:
- Does Judith teach me something about how one wins?
- Have I ever done things "Judith's way"?
- Is she a person I could emulate?
- What parts of Judith do I want to own? Disown?

What questions and problems does this still leave unanswered or "in process"?

CHAPTER 8

QUEEN ESTHER: GENOCIDE, FAITH, AND THE WHOLE MEGILLAH

The Book of Esther (entire text)

1:1–22	The King of Kings and his uppity queen
2:1–17	The royal talent search
3:1–15	Haman (a name to hiss at)
4:1–5:8	Esther's awakening
6:1–11	Haman's first comeuppance
7:1–10	Esther springs her trap
8:1–9:4	The sentence revoked
9:5–13	A problem of justice
9:20–29	Establishing Purim
10	Another happy ending

REFLECTION ON CHAPTER 8

In reading the story:
- What does the narrative tell us about Esther?
- How does she change or grow during the course of the story?
- What can you tell about her relationship with God?
- What kind of courage does she show compared to, say, Judith?

Self-reflection and learning:
- Can I identify with Esther?
- Is she a person I can admire or emulate?
- What parts of Esther do I want to own? Disown?
- What troubling questions does she raise for me?

What questions and problems does this still leave unanswered or "in process"?

She comes with mother's kindnesses

Kingsfold

1 She comes with moth - er's kind - ness - es and bends to touch and heal.
2 She comes with work - er's faith - ful - ness to sow and reap and spin.
3 She comes, a child of hum - ble - ness and trust is in her eyes,
4 She comes with sis - ter's care - ful - ness, strong to sup - port and bind,

1 She gives her heart a - way in love for those who can - not feel.
2 She bends her back in com - mon task to gath - er har - vest in.
3 and through them all of life ap - pears in won - der - ing sur - prise.
4 her voice will speak for jus - tice' sake, and peace is in her mind.

1 She comes with lov - er's ten - der - ness to an - swer love's ap - peal,
2 She comes with art - ist's joy - ful - ness to make and shape and sing,
3 She comes, a friend who walks the road, to share what each day brings.
4 She comes with pow - er like the night and glo - ry like the day,

1 she gives her bod - y with her heart to make her pas - sion real.
2 she gives her hands and from them grows a free and love - ly thing.
3 In grief, her tears rain down with ours; in joy, her laugh - ter rings.
4 her reign is in the heart of things. O come to us and stay.

Music: *Kingsfold*, English melody; adapt. and harm. Ralph Vaughan Williams (1872–1958). Words: Kathy Galloway (v. 3b by M. R. Ritley).

MFL 17 from **Music for Liturgy**, 2nd Edition (1999) published by St. Gregory of Nyssa Episcopal Church, 500 DeHaro Street, San Francisco, CA 94107. Visit our website: **www.saintgregorys.org**

NOTES

CHAPTER 1

1. Some readers may recognize the term B.C. but not B.C.E. Briefly, B.C. and A.D. were designations used by Christian writers to indicate years Before Christ (B.C.), or in the Year of the Lord (Anno Domini, or A.D.) It took until the twentieth century for western Christians to recognize that this way of reckoning time was offensive to people of other faiths, since Jews, Muslims, and Buddhists all have their own systems of numbering the years. Scholars began to use the designations C.E. and B.C.E. (meaning Christian Era and Before the Christian Era), but soon saw that this wasn't really any easier to justify. The current usage interprets these initials as Common Era, and Before the Common Era. And no, you don't have to recalculate anything: the dates are exactly the same as the old B.C. and A.D. ones.

2. This is not universally true, by the way. There were people like Gregory of Nyssa, a fourth-century bishop from what is now modern-day Turkey, who believed that the Incarnation would have happened whether humanity had sinned or not. If God loved humanity as deeply as God does, God would want to share the entire experience that humanity has, including being born and dying. Unfortunately, this has always been a minority view.

CHAPTER 2

3. Actually, the text says "Abram" and "Sarai" at this point; God doesn't change their names to Abraham and Sarah until much later in the story. To avoid confusion, however, I'll refer to them by their later, and better-recognized names throughout.

4. Mary Douglas, *Purity and Danger: An Analysis of Concepts of Pollution and Taboo* (London: Routledge and Kegan Paul, 1978.)

CHAPTER 3

5. A much fuller explanation of scenes of this type, and the ways in which biblical storytellers use them can be found in Robert Alter's *The Art of Biblical Narrative*. (Robert Alter, *The Art of Biblical Narrative* [New York: Basic Books, 1981.]) While it's not necessary to understanding the chapter that follows, it's a small, well-written book that will well repay the reading.

6. What all this tells us, probably, is that for a very long time there was a relationship between the Israelites and the Ishmaelites that involved sharing pasture land and wells. The Hagar story was one of the ways in which both groups established their rights to these pastures and wells. Eventually, the groups separated, and at that point the remainder of Hagar's and the Ishmaelites' story was edited out. But what we're left with is extraordinary.

7. Although the story is fairly traditional in some Sufi orders, especially among women, the telling is my own. I am, however, particularly indebted to my teacher, the late André Fikri, and to the late Mira Halaby, both of whom told versions of the story to me.

CHAPTER 4

8. Wilfred Owen, *The Collected Poems of Wilfred Owen*, ed. C. Day Lewis (New York: New Directions, 1965).

CHAPTER 5

9. "Sisters, Sisters." Words and music by Irving Berlin. Copyright 1954.

10. Rachel calls the boy "son of my sorrow," but Jacob, possibly to avoid being reminded of Rachel's death each time he hears the boy's name, calls him "son of the south" instead.

11. See Hymn #661, "Georgetown," words by William Alexander Percy, in *The Hymnal 1982*.

CHAPTER 7

12. The nameless and ambiguous maid's presence and part in the story has led many lesbians to claim Judith as one of their own, and her maid as Judith's lover. However appealing this may seem to some readers, there really isn't anything in the narrative itself to tell us anything about Judith's sexual orientation. The text itself implies that Judith (like the widow Anna in Luke 2:36–38) is exercising a recognized and respected option to devote herself to

God, having technically completed her obligation to marry. It is an option that will be honored down the centuries in Christian tradition as well, particularly in Orthodox and Catholic tradition.

CHAPTER 8

13. *Megillah* is the Hebrew word for a scroll. On Purim, the whole scroll of Esther is read. Since it is a complicated story that wanders around a lot and leaves absolutely nothing out, it's almost overkill, especially when you have to listen to the whole thing. So "the whole megillah" (*gantse megillah* in Yiddish) means an explanation or story that goes on forever, or something very complicated.